# When QUILT DESIGNERS think *small*

# When

## QUILT DESIGNERS

## think *small*

Innovative quilt designs
to wear, give, or decorate your home

CREATIVE
PUBLISHING
international

**CHANHASSEN, MINNESOTA**
www.creativepub.com

Copyright © 2004
Creative Publishing international, Inc.
18705 Lake Drive East
Chanhassen, Minnesota 55317
1-800-328-3895
www.creativepub.com
All rights reserved

President/CEO: Michael Eleftheriou
Vice President/Publisher: Linda Ball
Vice President/Retail Sales: Kevin Haas

WHEN QUILT DESIGNERS THINK SMALL

Created by: The Editors of Creative Publishing international, Inc.

Executive Editor: Alison Brown Cerier
Managing Editor: Yen Le
Art Director/Designer: Lois Stanfield
Senior Editor: Linda Neubauer
Stylist: Joanne Wawra
Illustrator: M. Deborah Pierce
Photographer: Tate Carlson
Director of Production: Kim Gerber

Library of Congress Catloging-in-Publication Data
Number 2003063475

ISBN 1-58923-131-7

Printed by R R Donnelley:
 10 9 8 7 6 5 4 3 2 1

Creative Publishing international, Inc. offers a variety of
how-to books. For information write:
    Creative Publishing international, Inc.
      Subscriber Books
    18705 Lake Drive East
    Chanhassen, MN 55317

ACKNOWLEDGEMENTS

Special thanks to the following designers:

Denise Bielick
Debbie Bowles
Barbara Boyd
Janis Bullis
Patricia Converse
Phyllis Dobbs
Karen Bailey Earith
Laura Murray
Susan Stein
Julann Windsperger

# CONTENTS

# Introduction

*We recently asked the owner* of a wonderful quilt shop what kinds of quilt projects are most popular among her customers. She said people often ask for quilt projects that are small in size, so they can be completed in a weekend, a day, or an evening. After all, lives are busy, and a queen-sized bed quilt or a large wall hanging can take weeks of patience and attention. We decided to challenge ten noted quilt designers to think small. They dazzled us with projects that are not only small in size, but huge in creativity. The designers used a wide range of quilting styles and embellishments in very inventive ways to make things that people could really use— wearables, home décor items, and great gifts. This book shares their original quilt concepts with you.

Have you ever foiled velvet or made feathers out of fabric? Try Laura Murray's Foiled Velvet Pillow or Julann Windsperger's Feathered Patchwork Bag. Debbie Bowles designed a VIP Triangle Scrap Quilt that introduces you to her unique technique for using those Very Important (leftover) Pieces. Some of the projects feature art fabrics, such as Susan Stein's Fabric Collage Wall Hanging, or creative handiwork, such as Phyllis Dobbs's Mini Art Wall Quilt. If you want to quilt a gift for a special friend, you'll enjoy Patricia Converse's Dragonfly Glasses Case or Janis Bullis's quilted game boards. Accompany your gift with Karen Bailey Earith's Paper-pieced Greeting Cards. If you are feeling a bit nostalgic, perhaps Barbara Boyd's Vintage Hankie Pillow or Denise Bielick's Crazy Quilted Photo Frame is the project for you.

The twenty projects in this book are fun, quick, and easy. Many can be made with fabrics you have on hand for those times you decide on the spur of the moment to quilt something. Go ahead and try something new—a small project is a great chance to explore.

Enjoy thinking and quilting small!

—*The Editors of Creative Publishing international*

# DRAGONFLY
## *Glasses Case*

by Patricia Converse

*Dragonflies* are common above the fields and brooks around Patricia's rural Pennsylvania home. She enjoys watching them dart and hover. One morning in July, perhaps sensing her admiration, a particularly bold dragonfly settled on her finger. It stayed there long enough for her to study its marvelous colors and design, as if knowing that she would appliqué its image onto one of her quilted creations. Patricia designed this elegant case with its beaded chain—just the thing to hold a quilter's glasses.

Glasses Case
3" × 6" *(7.5 × 15 cm)*
*Satin stitch appliqué, free-motion quilting, beading*

## MATERIALS

**Two coordinating fabrics for background and lining, 10" × 10" (25.5 × 25.5 cm) of each**

**Two coordinating fabrics for wings, 2" × 6" (5 × 15 cm) of each**

**Paper-backed fusible web, 10" × 15" (25.5 × 38 cm)**

**Tear-away stabilizer, 10" × 15" (25.5 × 38 cm)**

**Rayon thread to coordinate with the wing fabric for appliqué satin stitching**

**Appliqué presser foot**

**Walking foot**

**Cotton thread to coordinate with background fabric for construction and quilting**

**Light cotton batting, 10" × 15" (25.5 × 38 cm)**

**Quilter's safety pins**

**#8 pearl cotton for necklace**

**16" (40.5 cm) strand of beads in each of these colors and sizes: black 8 mm, black 10 mm, yellow aurora borealis 4 mm, red aurora borealis 6 mm**

**Hand needle for beading**

## Instructions

1   Wash, dry, and press all the fabrics. Shrink the batting according to the manufacturer's directions, if desired.

2   Trace the glasses case patterns on pages 12 and 13; cut out. Place the pattern pieces on the right side of the background fabric, right side up, and trace around them.

3   Trace the wing patterns; cut out. Cut two pieces of paper-backed fusible web, each 1¾" × 5¾" (4.5 cm × 14.5 cm). Trace the wings onto the paper backing of the fusible web. Fuse the web to the wrong side of the wing fabric, following the manufacturer's directions. Cut out the wings; remove the paper backing.

4   Fuse the wings to the glasses case front, using the pattern for placement. The upper wings should overlap the lower wings slightly. Note that the wing edges must be at least ⅜" (1 cm) from the case edges to allow for seams.

5   Place a 10" (25.5 cm) square of tear-away stabilizer behind the background fabric. Thread the machine with rayon thread, and set your machine for a scant ⅛" (3 mm) wide satin stitch. Stitch the lower wings in place, beginning and ending at the points where they meet the upper wings. Pull thread tails to the back; knot and cut.

6   Stitch the upper wings, beginning at the center and covering the end stitches of the lower wings. Straight-stitch vein lines onto the wings as desired. Pull thread ends to the back; knot and cut. Carefully remove the stabilizer. Press lightly.

7 Smooth the background fabric over a 10" (25.5 cm) square of batting. Baste it in place using safety pins. Thread the machine with black cotton thread and attach a walking foot; set for a short straight stitch. Stitch tightly around the outer edge of the wings, creating a shadow effect.

8 Attach a darning or free-motion embroidery foot; thread the machine with cotton thread to coordinate with the background fabric. Using free-motion quilting techniques, stitch loopy designs over the front and back of the case, suggesting the flight path of the dragonfly.

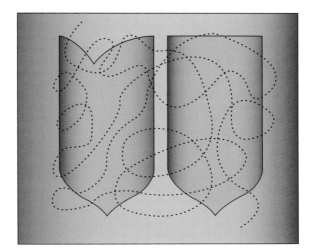

9 Cut out the case front and back on the marked lines. Place the pattern pieces on the wrong side of the lining fabric and cut them out.

10 Pin the lining front to the case front along the top edge, right sides together. Stitch ¼" (6 mm) seam. Repeat with the back pieces. Clip up to the stitches at the point of the front seam.

11 Open the pieces. Pin the front to the back, right sides together, aligning the edges and matching the seams. Stitch ¼" (6 mm) seam, leaving an opening in the lining for turning. Turn right side out.

## DESIGNER'S TIP

*When you appliqué, the stitches should always be perpendicular to the edge of the design piece. Practice satin stitching on a sharp curve. To keep the stitching perpendicular to the edge as you round a corner, stop with the needle down in the fabric on the outside stitch (dots), lift the presser foot, turn the project slightly, lower the presser foot, and continue. Pivot in this manner as often as necessary to suit the sharpness of the curve.*

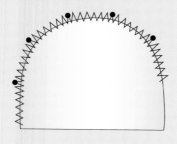

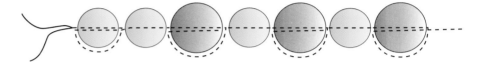

12   Thread a hand needle with a double black thread; knot the end. Insert the needle through the opening in the lining, and bring it through to the right side at the tail-end of the dragonfly body, as indicated on the pattern. Add a yellow bead and backstitch. Add a yellow bead and a black 8 mm bead; backstitch. Repeat twice. Add a black 8 mm bead; backstitch. Repeat. Add a black 10 mm bead; backstitch. Repeat. Bring thread to inside and knot.

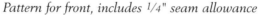

13   Thread a needle with a double strand of pearl cotton; knot the end. Bring the needle to the right side at the bottom point of the case. String one black 10 mm bead, three

*Pattern for front, includes ¹/₄" seam allowance*

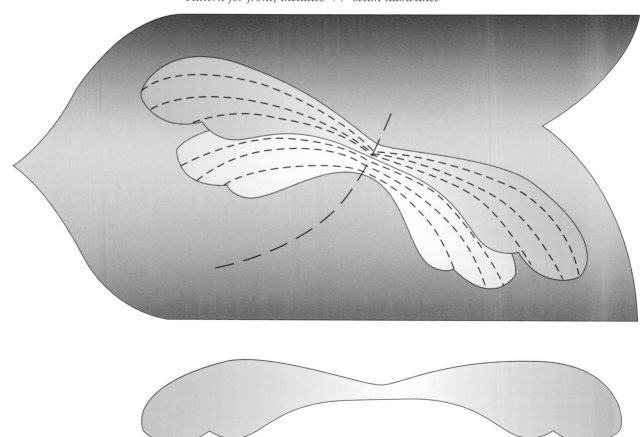

yellow, one red, and three yellow. Make a knot below the last bead large enough to keep the beads from slipping off.

14  Bring a second double strand of pearl cotton from the inside through the black bead. Add seven yellow beads and knot. Repeat for a third string of beads. Trim the tails to a pleasing length, and comb them with a pin to open the fibers.

15  Thread the needle with a double strand of pearl cotton about 35" (89 cm) long; make a large knot in the end. Bring the thread to the outside at the upper edge side seam. String a pleasing pattern of assorted beads until the necklace is the desired length. Bring the needle to the inside at the opposite upper edge seam and knot securely.

16  Slipstitch the lining opening closed. Push the lining inside the case.

*Pattern for back, includes 1/4" seam allowance*

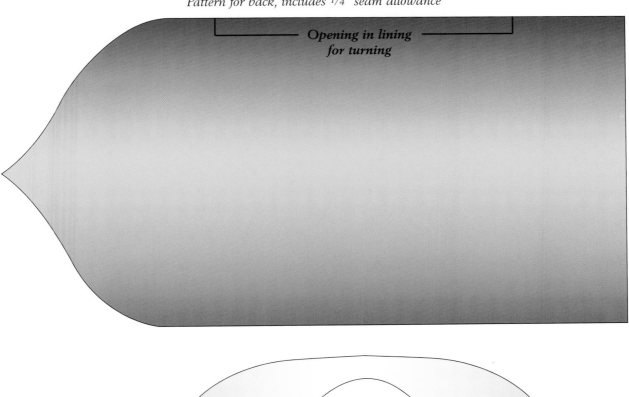

**Opening in lining
for turning**

# FEATHERED
# *Patchwork Bag*

by Julann Windsperger

*One bright-blue spring day*, Julann was watching the craziness of the birds, just back from their migrations, and was inspired to figure out a way to turn fabrics into feathers. She used the fabric feathers to accent a bright blue handbag of contemporary crazy patchwork. The technique for making the background fabric is a wonderful exercise in creative exploration. The instructions will make enough art fabric that you will have extra for other projects, such as a stole or vest.

Handbag
*8" × 11" (20.5 × 28 cm)*
*Contemporary crazy patchwork,*
*beading, couching, fabric "sculpture"*

## MATERIALS

**Four to six coordinating print fabrics, ¼ yd. (0.25 m) of each**

**Decorative yarns**

**1¼ yd. (1.15 m) background fabric in a solid-type sky blue color**

**¼ yd. (0.25 m) gold metallic fabric**

**Flannel for "batting"**

**Armo Press Soft 50/50 for quilt backing**

**Quilter's safety pins**

**Thread to match background**

**Paper-backed fusible web**

**Variegated thread**

**Beads**

**Metal button**

**Fine gauge craft wire**

## Instructions

1   Wash, dry, and press all the fabrics.

2   Cut 3" (7.5 cm) strips of each of the coordinating print fabrics; cut them into squares. Sew the squares together in random order into six rows of six squares each; press all the seam allowances of each row in one direction. Then stitch the rows together, alternating the direction of the seam allowances; arrange the rows so same fabrics are not adjacent to each other.

3   Couch decorative yarns over the surface of the pieced fabric in wavy lines at various angles, using three-stitch zigzag and variegated thread. Layer yarns to create more texture and color.

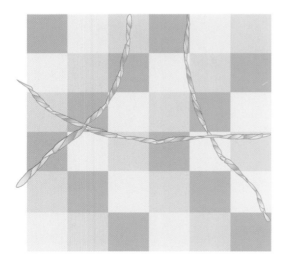

4    Cut three 1½" (3.8 cm) strips from the entire width of the background fabric. Cut the pieced fabric from one edge to another in a straight line at any angle. Stitch the pieces to either side of a background strip; press the seams toward the strip. Repeat this step twice at different angles, crossing the first strip if desired.

### DESIGNER'S TIP

*The contemporary crazy patchwork described in this project can be used to create a base fabric for almost any other project you have in mind—a vest, pillow cover, placemats, tote bag, or album cover. It is a good way to use small pieces of fabrics you may have left over from other quilts, as long as they share similar colors. The strips of background fabric and accent fabric bring your assortment of patchwork pieces into a cohesive grouping.*

5    Cut three 1" (2.5 cm) strips from the entire width of the gold metallic fabric. Cut the fabric and insert a gold strip as in step 4 three times.

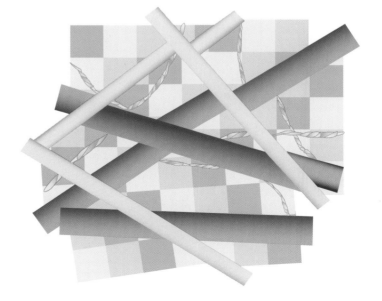

6    Draw an 8" (20.5 cm) square on paper for the bag flap pattern. Redraw the lower edge at a slant from the lower left corner to the halfway mark on the right side. Cut away and discard the lower right triangle. Using the pattern, chalk out the area of the pieced fabric that you want to use for the bag flap. Reserve the rest for another project.

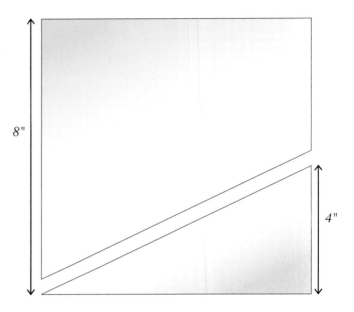

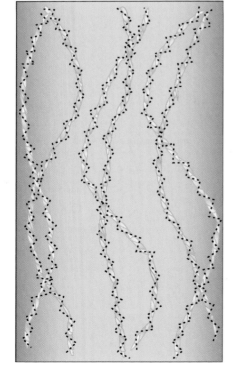

7    Cut a 13" × 25" (33 × 63.5 cm) rectangle of background fabric. Cut 15" × 27" (38 × 68.5 cm) rectangles of Armo Press Soft and flannel. Layer and pin-baste the pieces, sandwiching the flannel in the middle.

8    Chalk out a 9" × 21" (23 × 53.5 cm) area for the bag body. Chalk wavy intersecting lines over the rectangle. Couch yarns over the lines, using three-stitch zigzag and variegated thread. Cut the bag body layers 9" × 21" (23 × 53.5 cm).

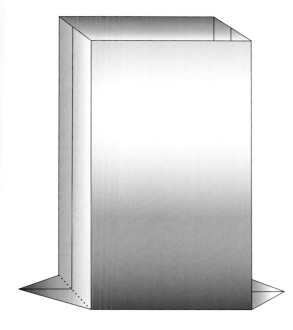

9 Cut two 1½" × 4" (3.8 × 10 cm) rectangles of one of the piecing fabrics; fuse them wrong sides together. Cut out the small feather shape, using the appliqué pattern (page 21). Cut the veins up close to the center line. Repeat for as many feathers as you want. Secure them to the purse front by stitching twice down the center. Hand-stitch beads at the tops.

10 Fold the purse front in half, right sides together. Stitch the sides. Fold out paper-bag corners and stitch ¾" (2 cm) from the point.

11 Cut a 9" × 21" (23 × 53.5 cm) rectangle of the background fabric for the lining. Cut and line a rectangle of pieced fabric for an inner pocket if desired; topstitch it to one side of the lining.

12 Stitch the lining as in step 10. Slip the lining inside the bag, wrong sides together. Baste ⅛" (3 mm) from the upper edge.

13 Cut a strip of the background fabric 3" (7.5 cm) wide, for binding. Fold the strip in half lengthwise. Pin the raw edges to the upper edge of the bag, on the lining side; lap the ends at the back.

14 Stitch ½" (1.3 cm) from the upper edge. Wrap the binding snugly over the raw edges, covering the stitching line on the outside. Pin in place. Stitch in the ditch.

15 Cut a 10" (25.5 cm) square of the pieced fabric in the area designated for the flap. Layer it over squares of flannel and Armo Press Soft. Stitch a grid of wavy lines about 1" (2.5 cm) apart in both directions, using variegated thread.

16 Cut out the flap, using the pattern drawn in step 6. Stitch one or two feathers to the flap, as in step 9. Also cut a flap lining from the background fabric.

17  Place the flap and lining wrong sides together. Stitch the sides and slanted edge in a ½" (1.3 cm) seam, beginning and ending 1" (2.5 cm) from the upper straight edge; leave the straight upper edge open. Trim corners diagonally; turn right side out.

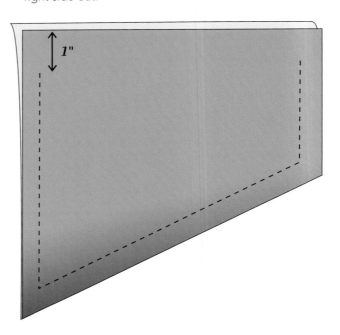

18  Make five small feathers for hanging along the flap front edge. Stitch down the center of the feather from the top; turn the feather around and stitch back to the beginning. Leave long thread tails. String beads onto the thread tails and then stitch the feathers to the flap, knotting the tails securely between the flap layers.

19  Stitch the flap front to the bag back, right sides together, stitching just below the binding. Turn under the lining and hand-stitch to the inside of the bag.

20  Cut a 3½" × 44" (9 × 112 cm) strip of the background fabric for the strap. Cut a strip of flannel 1¼" × 43" (3.2 × 109 cm). Place the flannel over the wrong side of the strap 1" (2.5 cm) from one side and ½" (1.3 cm) from each end. Press under the strap ends ½" (1.3 cm). Press the 1" (2.5 cm) side in over the flannel. Press under the other side ½" (1.3 cm), then ¾" (2 cm), encasing the flannel. Edgestitch down the inner fold.

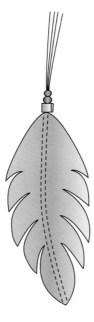

21  Stitch three gentle wavy lines down the length of the strap, using variegated thread. Center the strap ends over the bag side seams and stitch in place.

22  To make the wired feathers, fuse a wire between the fabric layers down the center of the feather. Leave a long tail of excess wire at the connecting end. Zigzag over the wire, using a short narrow stitch setting. Slip beads onto the wire. Form a loop in the wire for attaching the feather. Coil the wire end around a skewer or small knitting needle to form a tendril. Make several large and small wired feathers.

23  Stitch the metal button to the base of the strap on the right side of the bag. Hand-stitch the wired feathers under the button.

*Feather Patterns*

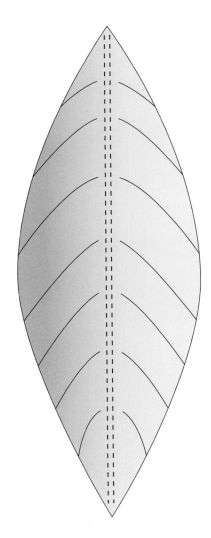

# PHOTO
# *Print Tote*

by Denise Bielick

*Printable fabric* has opened up all kinds of possibilities for quilters. Like most parents, Denise takes many photos of her children. Rather than hide them away in an album, she printed some of her favorites on fabric and stitched the blocks into a quilted tote that is used and admired every day. She used a subdued color scheme so the photos would take center stage. Being a soccer mom, Denise has also made a tote featuring photos of her kids in action on the field, using team colors for the sashing and sides. Paper piecing makes the sashing go together quickly and accurately. A photo tote would be a special Mother's Day gift for any proud mother or grandmother.

Tote Bag
*16" × 18" × 4" (40.5 × 46 × 10 cm)*
*Computer printing on fabric, paper piecing*

## MATERIALS

**Four sheets of computer printer fabric**

**Eight photos**

**Computer with photo editing software, scanner, and inkjet color printer**

**1½ yd. (1.4 m) large floral print fabric for lining, sides, bottom, and binding**

**½ yd. (0.5 m) yellow fabric for center squares of sashing stars and border**

**⅓ yd. (0.32 m) small pink floral fabric for sashing**

**Fat ¼ yd. green fabric for sashing stars**

**Fat ¼ yd. blue fabric for sashing stars**

**Scrap of pink fabric for center stars**

**Foundation paper**

**Lightweight stable batting: 20" × 40" (51 × 102 cm) for main body of tote, two 8" × 21" (20.5 × 53.5 cm) for sides**

**60" (152.5 cm) ecru cotton webbing, 1" (2.5 cm) wide, for handle**

**Two pieces of mat board, 3½" × 16" (9 × 40.5 cm)**

## Instructions

*1*   Scan the photos and size them to print 5" (12.7 cm) wide and 5¾" (14.5 cm) high. The finished size will be 4½" × 5¼" (11.5 × 13.2 cm). Using photo editing software, place two images ½" (1.3 cm) apart on a document in landscape position, allowing room for seam allowances. Print the photos on printable fabric, following the manufacturer's directions. Cut out the photos 5" × 5¾" (12.7 × 14.5 cm).

*2*   Wash, dry, and press the remaining fabrics. Shrink the batting, following the manufacturer's directions, if desired. From the large floral, cut a 20" × 40" (51 × 102 cm) rectangle for the main backing, a 4½" × 17" (11.5 × 43 cm) rectangle for the outer bottom, two 4½" × 18½" (11.5 × 47.3 cm) rectangles for the outer sides, two 8" × 21" (20.5 × 53.5 cm) rectangles for the backing sides, and a 2" (5 cm) binding strip.

*3*   Cut twenty-six 2" (5 cm) squares, eight 2" × 5" (5 × 12.7 cm) rectangles, and eight 2" × 5¾" (5 × 14.5 cm) rectangles from the yellow fabric. The remaining fabrics will be used for paper piecing the sashing units. Cut each piece at least ½" (1.3 cm) larger than the area it is to cover, as described in steps 4 to 6.

*4*   Copy the sashing unit patterns (pages 26 and 27) onto foundation paper. Using pattern A, make 16 units with yellow fabric for #1 and green fabric for #2 and #3. Make 8 units with yellow for #1 and blue fabric for #2 and #3. Trim the units ¼" beyond the outer line. See page 27 for paper-piecing instructions.

5   Make twelve units, using pattern B; use the pink print fabric
    for #1 and blue fabric for #2 and #3. For eight of the units,
    use green fabric for #4 and #5; for the remaining four, use
    pink fabric.

6   Repeat step 5 using pattern C. Following the diagram,
    stitch each row of the tote together, using ¼" seams.
    Prepare one set for the front and one for the back
    of the tote.

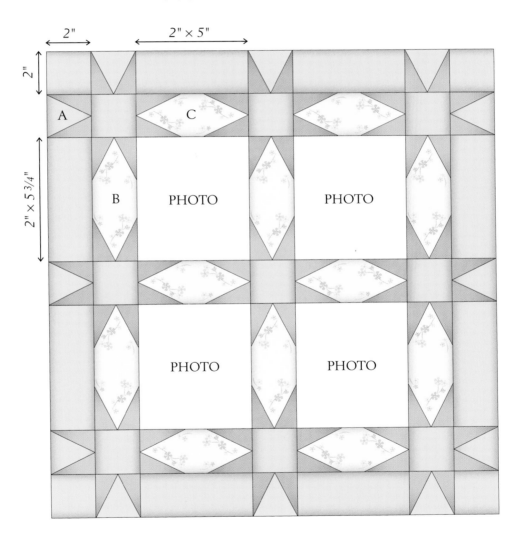

7   Stitch one side of the 4½" × 17" (11.5 × 43 cm) rectangle to
    the bottom of the front. Stitch the other side to the bottom
    of the back.

## DESIGNER'S TIP

*Conserve your foundation paper and shorten your stitching time. Follow the diagrams to trace the patterns onto five 8¹/₂" × 11" (21.8 × 28 cm) sheets of foundation paper. Cut the patterns into strips or groups to work on several at a time in assembly line fashion. Cut the necessary fabric pieces to their approximate sizes and stack them next to the machine. When you finish stitching, move to the cutting board to cut them all apart.*

| A | A | A | A |
|---|---|---|---|
| A | A | A | A |
| A | A | A | A |
| A | A | A | A |
| A | A | A | A |

| A | B |
|---|---|
| A | B |
| A | B |
| A | B |
|   | B |

| C | B |
|---|---|
|   | B |
|   | B |
| C | B |
|   | B |

| C | B |
|---|---|
|   | B |
|   | C |
| C | C |
|   | C |

| C | C | C | C |
|---|---|---|---|
| C | C | C | C |

8  Layer and baste the backing, batting, and quilt top. Stitch in the ditch around the photos and stars and bottom seams. Stitch quilting lines down the center of the bottom and 1" (2.5 cm) from each side of center. Trim off the excess batting and backing.

9  Layer and baste the tote side pieces. Stitch quilting lines down the center and 1" (2.5 cm) from each side of center. Trim off the excess batting and backing.

10  Stitch the sides to the tote, using set-in-seaming. Finish the raw edges with zigzag stitches or by serging.

11  Press the binding strip in half, wrong sides together. Stitch the binding to the right side of the upper edge. Turn to the inside and hand-stitch in place.

12  Cut the webbing in half. Fold under ½" (1.3 cm) on the ends and stitch. Attach the ends to the inside of the tote behind the corner stars, stitching over the previous quilting stitches.

13  Glue the two pieces of mat board together. Adhere fabric to one side, wrapping onto the other side. Place in the bottom of the tote for stability.

*Sashing Unit Patterns*

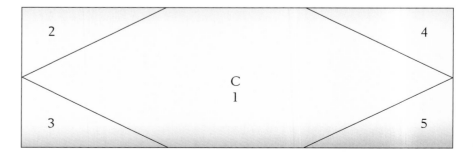

## GENERAL PAPER PIECING INSTRUCTIONS

Follow these steps to create each of the units for the tote sashing or to create the greeting card inserts on page 39.

1   Center the first fabric piece over section #1, right side up. Place the second piece over the first, right sides together, roughly aligning the raw edges about 1/4" (6 mm) from their shared stitching line. Check to see that fabric #2 will cover its area when turned into position. Pin if necessary.

2   Flip the pattern over, so the fabrics are on the underside. Stitch on the shared stitching line, beginning and ending two stitches beyond the line.

3   Flip the pattern over, and finger-press fabric #2 into position. Trim the seam allowances to 1/4" (6 mm). Place the third piece over the first two, right sides together, roughly aligning the shared stitching line between #1 and #3; check the position. Repeat step 2 on the second stitching line.

4   Continue adding sections in order as numbered. Stitch around the entire pattern just outside the outer stitching line. Trim off the excess fabric 1/4" beyond the stitching line. Carefully tear away the paper.

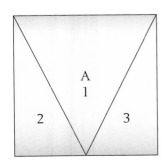

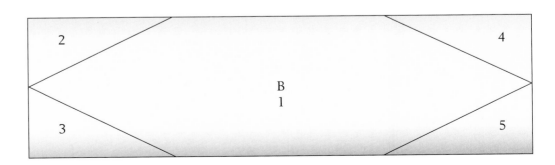

# ENGINEER
## *Quilted Vest*

by Susan Stein

*Inspiration* for this child-sized engineer's vest was all around Susan. Her husband has been a "train nut" since he was a boy. On weekends, he runs full-size tourist trains, and he has filled their basement with model trains. All of their grandchildren have striped overalls and caps. Soon they will all be chugging around the house in their new engineer vests. Each block of the quilted strip around the lower edge of the vest is a different colored boxcar, pulled by a blue locomotive with a red caboose bringing up the rear. Susan found the authentic patches for the vest at a railroad museum.

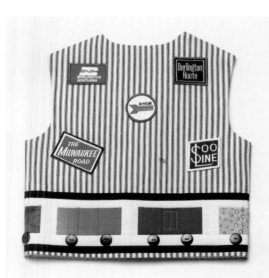

Quilted Vest
*30" × 4" (76 × 10 cm) quilted train*
*Conventional piecing*

## MATERIALS

**Vest pattern with straight lower edges, such as Butterick 3792**

**Blue ticking stripe fabric**

**Muslin for lining**

**Red bandanna**

**Railroad patches**

**Scraps of fabric for train cars, locomotive, and caboose**

**¼ yd. (0.25 m) background fabric**

**¾" (2 cm) black buttons for wheels, two for each car**

**Strip of lightweight batting, 3½" (9 cm) wide**

**Black, single-fold bias tape, ½" (1.3 cm) wide**

**Walking foot**

**Thread**

## Instructions

1   Wash, dry, and press all the fabrics. Shrink the batting according to the manufacturer's directions, if desired.

2   Cut out the vest and lining. Sew the vest side seams together, straightening the seam if it is curved. Press the seam allowances open.

3   Cut out a pocket from the ticking. Press under the top hem; press under the sides and bottom along the seamlines. Stitch a railroad patch to the center of the pocket. Stitch the pocket to the vest along the sides and bottom.

4   Cut the bandanna into quarters; tuck one quarter into the pocket, making sure all the raw edges are inside the pocket. Stitch across the top of the pocket, securing the bandanna.

5   Follow the diagrams to cut colored and background pieces for the locomotive, boxcars, and caboose. The measurements on the diagrams include ¼" seam allowances on all sides.

6   Stitch together the pieces for the locomotive, boxcars, and caboose, working in the units indicated on the locomotive diagram. Press seam allowances toward the colored fabrics whenever possible.

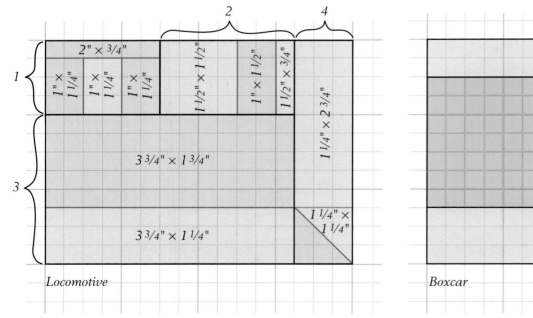

Locomotive

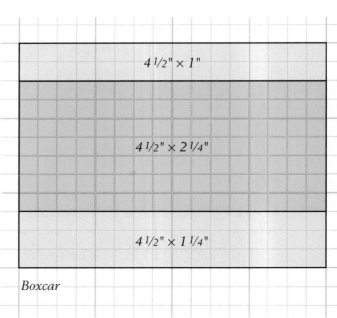

Boxcar

## DESIGNER'S TIP

*Accurate right triangles of any size are easy to make using this triangle-square method. For the cowcatcher at the front of the locomotive, cut a 2" (5 cm) square of background fabric and a 2" (5 cm) square of blue fabric. Place the squares right sides together, and stitch diagonally corner to corner. Cut off excess fabric 1/4" (6 mm) from one side of the stitching line. Press the seam allowances to one side and trim the square down to 1 1/4" (3.2 cm).*

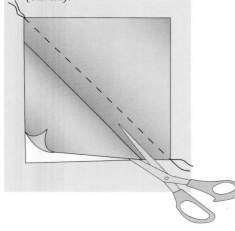

| 1 1/2" × 1" | 1 3/4" × 1" | 1 3/4" × 1" |
|---|---|---|

4" × 2 1/4"

4" × 1 1/4"

Caboose

7   Place the train blocks near the lower edge of the vest, spaced evenly about 1" (2.5 cm) apart. Cut 3½" (9 cm) high background rectangles to fit the spaces between cars, adding ½" (1.3 cm) for seam allowances. Include spacers for the front edges, allowing room for buttons and buttonholes, if desired. Connect the train blocks and spacers. Press seam allowances toward the spacers.

8   Place the batting strip under the train strip, and layer them both over the vest near the lower seamline; pin. Center ½" (1.3 cm) bias tape over the top and bottom edges of the strip. Using a walking foot, topstitch along both edges of the bias tape, securing the train strip to the vest.

9   Quilt around the train cars. Add details as desired. Stitch additional railroad patches to the front and back of the vest, as desired.

10   Sew the vest and lining together, following the pattern directions. If the pattern uses a side seam opening to finish the vest, transfer those directions to the shoulder seam, instead.

11   Stitch buttons below the locomotive, boxcars, and caboose for wheels.

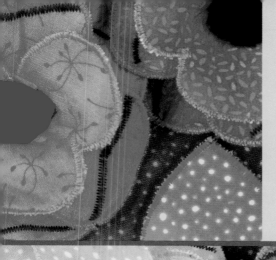

# 3-D FLOWERS
# *Hat Box*

by Janis Bullis

*Dimensional flowers* in bold, neon colors decorate the top of a fabric-covered hat box. Perfect for storing small keepsakes, balls of yarn, sewing supplies, doll clothes, or even a hat, this box brightens up the room just by being there! Janis's technique for making three-dimensional flowers is fun and easy. You can also use the flowers to adorn gift bags, curtain tiebacks, or even a hat to put in the box.

Hat Box
3<sup>1</sup>/2" × 5" × 1<sup>1</sup>/4" (9 × 12.7 × 3.2 cm) *each flower*
*Satin stitching*

## MATERIALS

Cardboard or wood box with lid

Fabric to cover box

Three coordinating fabrics for flowers

Green fabric for leaves

Lightweight cotton quilt batting

Paper-backed fusible web

Lightweight nonwoven fusible interfacing, optional

Acrylic pompoms, ³/4" (2 cm) diameter

Thread in colors to match flowers and leaves, plus black

Removable fabric marking pen

Fabric glue

## DESIGNER'S TIP

*The simplest and least messy method for covering a sturdy cardboard box with fabric is with paper-backed fusible web. You may want to make yourself paper patterns for the box and lid first before cutting the fabric. Allow extra fabric to wrap over the upper and lower edges to the inside. Trim and clip fabric as necessary to fit. Finish the box bottom with a piece of fabric cut to the exact size.*

## Instructions

1   Wash, dry, and press all the fabrics. Shrink the batting according to the manufacturer's directions, if desired.

2   Cut six 4½" (11.5 cm) squares each of petal fabric, interfacing, and fusible web; cut three 4" (10 cm) squares of batting for the flower petal rings. Cut two 4½" × 3" (11.5 × 7.5 cm) pieces each of leaf fabric, interfacing, and fusible web; cut a 4" × 2½" (10 × 6.5 cm) piece of batting for the leaf.

3   Fuse the interfacing to the wrong side of the fabric pieces, following the manufacturer's instructions. Then fuse the fusible web to the interfacing. Remove the paper backing.

4   Place a piece of batting over the wrong side of a piece of fabric; cover with another piece of fabric, right side up. Fuse the layers together, pressing from both sides. Repeat for each petal ring and the leaf.

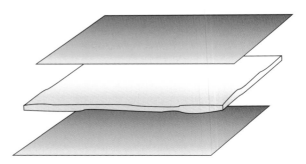

5   Trace the petal ring and leaf patterns onto one side of the fused fabrics; include the accent lines. Using matching thread and a short straight stitch, stitch around the outline of each petal ring and the leaf. Switch to black thread and satin stitch the accent line of the petals.

6   Trim the petal rings and leaf close to the stitching line. Using matching thread, satin stitch over the outer edge of each piece, allowing the stitches to wrap the raw edges. On the small upper petal ring, it is not necessary to satin stitch the tab and inner circle.

7   For the lower and center petal rings, fold each petal, right sides together, and stitch a shallow dart where indicated on the pattern. This will make the petals cup slightly.

8   For the upper petal ring, tuck the tab of the last petal under the first petal and hand-tack or glue in place, forming a funnel shape.

9   Hand-tack or glue the stack of petal rings together, staggering the petal placement. Attach a leaf to the underside. Glue a pompom to the center.

10   Make enough flowers to cover the box lid. Cover the box and lid with fabric, using fabric glue or fusible web. Glue the flowers to the box lid.

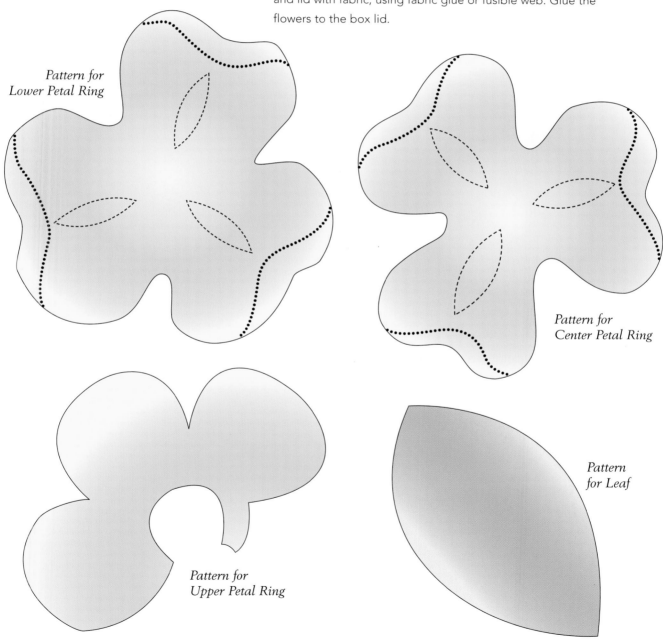

*Pattern for Lower Petal Ring*

*Pattern for Center Petal Ring*

*Pattern for Upper Petal Ring*

*Pattern for Leaf*

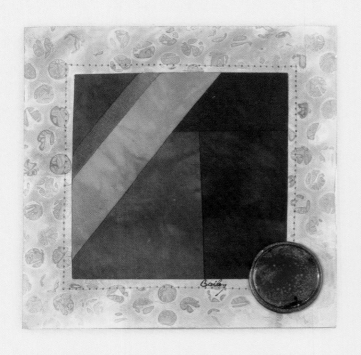

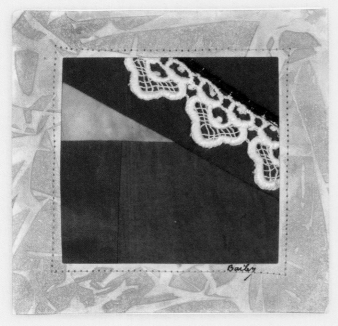

# PAPER-PIECED
# *Greeting Cards*

by Karen Bailey Earith

*Hand-dyed fabrics*, with their variable colors and visual depth, are treasures in themselves. Karen enjoys working them into her quilted projects, but finds that she cannot bear to toss away even the smallest scraps. By creating these contemporary, paper-pieced greeting cards, Karen found an artistic way to use the leftover pieces of her precious hand-dyed fabrics while sharing them with her friends. With the addition of unique found objects and watercolor painting, Karen calls this project "paper-piecing with a twist." Hand-made greeting cards always show extra thoughtfulness. These cards will also express your passion for quilting and show off watercolor painting skills you didn't know you had.

Greeting Cards
5" (12.7 cm) square
*Paper piecing, watercolor painting*

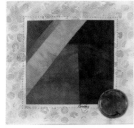

## MATERIALS

Assortment of hand-dyed
fabric scraps

Sewing machine with open-toe foot

Tracing paper or foundation paper

Small rotary cutter and cutting mat

Small see-through ruler with ¼"
(6 mm) marks

Coordinating thread

Iron

3" × 5" (7.5 × 12.7 cm) index card

Paper Creations® square window
white tri-fold cards

Dry pan watercolors

¾" (2 cm) wash paintbrush

Water

Bubble wrap, plastic wrap, or
tissue paper

Masking Magic™ 4½" × 5½"
(11.5 × 14 cm) sheets

Low-Loft® batting

¼" (6 mm) double sided
adhesive tape

Keep A Memory™ ACID-FREE
Sticky Dots™ adhesive tape

Assorted embellishments

## *Instructions*

1   Trace pattern A onto tracing paper or foundation paper.
Cut a piece of fabric for each section at least ½" (1.3 cm)
larger than the section. Following the general paper piecing
instructions on page 27, stitch the fabric pieces together to
complete the unit.

2   Repeat step 1 for pattern B. When the block is complete,
stitch a piece of lace over section #4.

3   Repeat step 1 for pattern C. Before attaching section #4,
cut a 3" (7.5 cm) square of contrasting fabric; fold it in half,
top to bottom. Fold the sides diagonally from the midpoint
of the first fold, creating a triangle (prairie point). Insert the
prairie point into the seam when attaching section #4, with
the folds facing up or down as desired.

4   Set the quilt blocks aside. Open a card and lay it flat. Cut
Masking Magic into ½" (1.3 cm) strips and adhere them
along the folds to protect areas not to be painted.

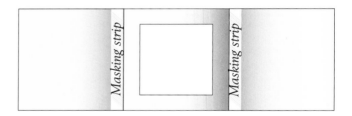

5   Lightly wet the frame area with a wet brush. Apply paint
randomly on the frame, layering two or three colors to
coordinate with the fabric. (Paint will dry lighter than in
the cake.)

6   Cover the wet paint with bubble wrap, plastic wrap, or
crumpled tissue paper; allow to dry. The colors will migrate
and form interesting textures as the cards dry. Remove the
covering when the paint is dry. Remove the masking strips.

7   Cut a piece of batting the same size as the pieced block.
Layer the batting, pieced block, and card frame. Stitch
around the card frame ⅛" (3 mm) from the opening, using
a medium to long straight stitch and coordinating thread.

8 Trim the fabric and batting to ¼" (6 mm). Place double-sided tape along the top, bottom, and right edges of the frame back. Fold the backing panel over to encase the quilted design.

9 Adhere small charms, old buttons, or other embellishments to the card front, using Sticky Dots.

*Pattern A*

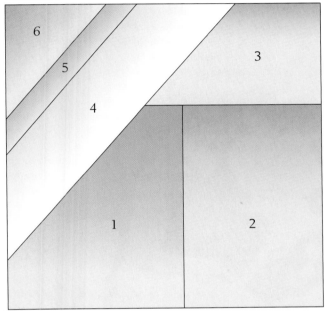

**DESIGNER'S TIP**

*Keep an index card next to your machine when you are paper piecing. After each seam, align the straight edge of the card to the stitching line and fold back the foundation paper to reveal the seam allowances. Use a small rotary cutting ruler to measure ¼" (1.3 cm) away from the stitching line, and trim the seam allowances, using a small rotary cutter and mat.*

*Pattern B*

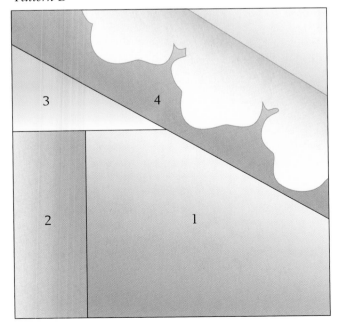

*Pattern C*

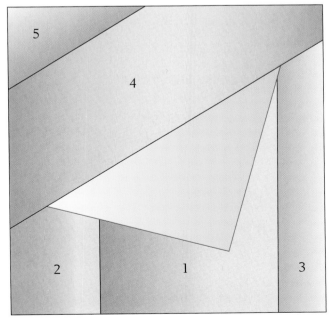

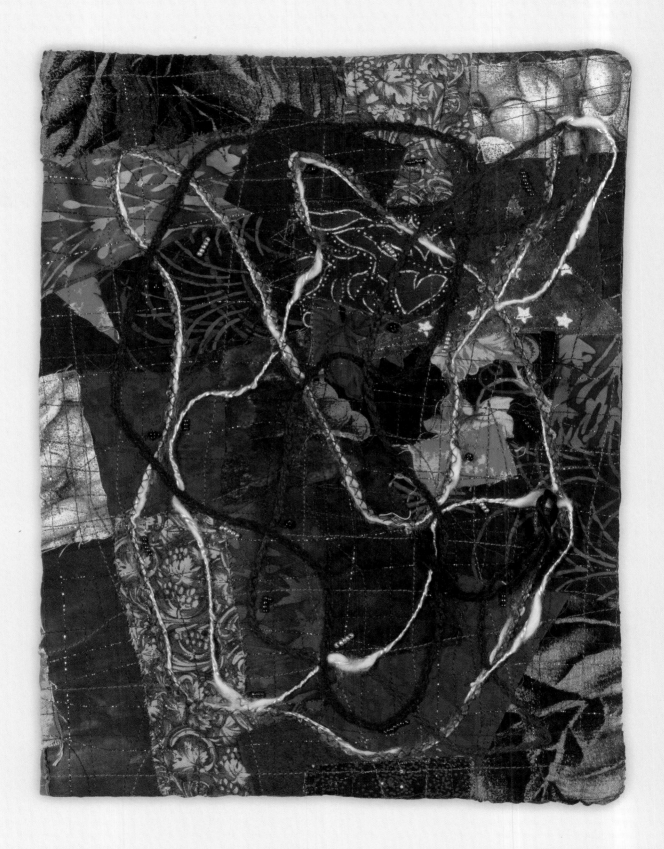

# FABRIC COLLAGE
## *Book Cover and Card Case*

by Karen Bailey Earith

*Fabric collage* that combines traditional and non-traditional fabrics, threads, and embellishments creates texture that just begs to be touched. Karen turned a fabulous fabric collage into covers for her organizer and business card case. The covers make her feel connected to her quilting studio wherever she may go, from a quilt show to the grocery store. You can also use the same method to create a cover for an appointment book, journal, Bible, address book, or credit-card case.

Book Cover and Business Card Case
*Make to your own specifications.*
*Fabric collage, couching, beading*

## Book Cover Instructions

1   Measure the front, spine, and back of the book with the book closed. Cut a rectangle of foundation fabric at least 2" (5 cm) larger in both directions. Arrange fabric scraps on the foundation fabric. Overlap edges by at least ¼" (6 mm) to cover the foundation completely.

2   Using a straight stitch, stitch back and forth over the fabric horizontally and vertically to create a grid. Space the stitching lines irregularly ¼" to ½" (6 mm to 1.3 cm) apart. Use several different threads including metallics for added interest. Continue stitching until all the fabric is anchored to the foundation.

3   Cut the fabric to the outer measurements of the book plus 1¼" (3.2 cm) in both directions for seam allowances and ease. Mark the exact size of the front cover. Couch yarns and decorative cords as desired within the marked area. Using a needle and thread, stitch beads to the front cover area as desired.

4   Cut a rectangle of lining the same size as the book cover. Cut two rectangles for the end flaps the same height as the book cover (top to bottom) and 9" (23 cm) wide. Fold the flaps in half lengthwise, wrong sides together; press.

### MATERIALS

½ yd. (0.5 m) or less foundation fabric

Assorted fabric scraps, 1" to 3" (2.5 to 7.5 cm), in a variety of color values and prints

½ yd. (0.5 m) coordinating fabric for lining and flaps

Assorted decorative threads

Assorted specialty yarns (about 3 yd. [2.75 m])

Assorted seed beads in black, green, and gold

Sewing machine with open-toe foot and couching foot

Rotary cutter, mat, ruler

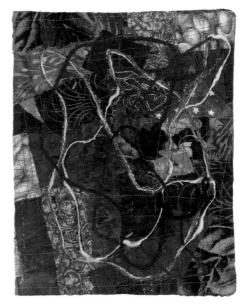

5   Place the cover right side up. Place a flap at each end of the cover, aligning the raw edges together. Place the lining piece right side down on top, matching raw edges. Pin.

6   Stitch around the outside edge with a 1/2" (1.3 cm) seam allowance, leaving a 3" (7.5 cm) opening along the bottom back edge for turning.

7   Trim the corners diagonally. Turn the cover right side out. Press the outer seamed edge. Slipstitch the opening closed. Insert the book.

## Card Case Instructions

1   Cut the foundation fabric 6½" × 7" (16.3 × 18 cm). Arrange fabric scraps on foundation fabric. Create the fabric collage as in steps 1 and 2 opposite. Trim case and lining to 5½" × 4¾" (14 × 12 cm).

2   Fold the case in half crosswise, right sides together. Stitch the sides with 1/4" (6 mm) seams. Repeat for the lining, leaving a 1½" (3.8 cm) opening on one side. Press the seam allowances open.

3   Slip the lining inside the case, right sides together, aligning the upper raw edges. Stitch a 1/4" (6 mm) seam. Turn right side out through the opening. Slipstitch the opening closed. Turn the lining into the case.

### DESIGNER'S TIP

*Temporary fabric adhesive in a convenient spray can is a great way to keep your fabric scraps in place until you have a chance to stitch them down. The adhesive is temporary. It can be washed away. Some brands actually diminish in time. The adhesive is also repositionable, so you can change your mind and rearrange the pieces. Place your scraps face down in a box and spray lightly. The box sides will catch any overspray.*

# PIECED STAR
## *Jewelry Roll*

by Phyllis Dobbs

*Strong colors and bold patterns* are always inspiring to Phyllis. She also loves the challenge of creating unique designs that are as useful as they are attractive. In this zippy little jewelry roll, she incorporated some simple piecework and added texture with the pieced star appliqué. Her designs often include hand embellishments like the blanket stitching that finishes the edges of the appliqué.

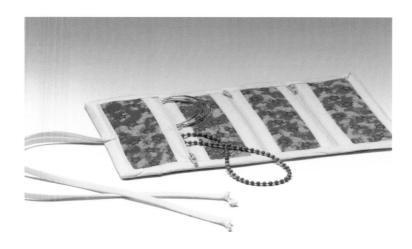

Jewelry Roll
*7" × 11¼" (18 × 28.7 cm)*
*Conventional piecing, fused appliqué, embroidery*

## MATERIALS

½ yd. (0.5 m) green print fabric

¼ yd. (0.25 m) yellow marbled fabric

⅛ yd. (0.15 m) pink tonal fabric

DMC six-strand cotton embroidery floss; bright green #907

Warm & Natural® needled cotton batting

Steam-A-Seam 2 fusible web

Three yellow zippers, 7" (18 cm)

Wide yellow double-fold bias tape

Narrow yellow double-fold bias tape

Bright green button

Yellow and green threads

Monofilament thread

## Instructions

1   Wash, dry, and press all the fabrics. Shrink the batting according to the manufacturer's directions, if desired.

2   Cut a 4½" (11.5 cm) square of yellow fabric (A). From the green fabric, cut two 1¾" × 4½" (4.5 × 11.5 cm) rectangles (B) and two 6½" × 7" (16.3 × 18 cm) rectangles (C) for the front. For the backing and inside, cut one 16½" × 7" (41.8 × 18 cm) rectangle and four 2¼" × 7" (6 × 18 cm) rectangles (D). Using the diamond pattern for the star, cut eight pink pieces. These measurements and pattern include ¼" (6 mm) seam allowances.

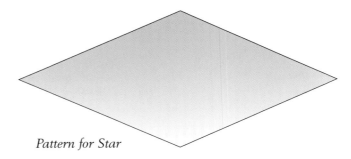

*Pattern for Star*

3   Cut three rectangles of batting: one 16½" × 7" (41.8 × 18 cm) and two 2¼" × 7" (6 × 18 cm).

4   Stitch the B rectangles to opposite sides of the A square, using ¼" (6 mm) seam allowances. Press the seam allowances away from the center.

5　Stitch the 7" (18 cm) sides of the C rectangles to opposite sides of the pieced unit. Press the seam allowances away from the center.

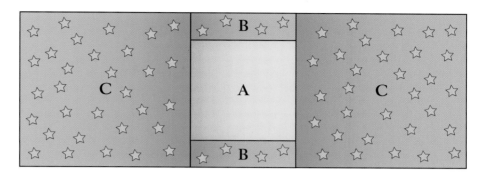

6　Stitch two diamonds together along one side. Repeat for the remaining three pairs. Then stitch two 2-diamond units together, aligning the seams. Repeat with the other two units.

7　Press the seam allowances in each set in one direction. Stitch the two sets together, aligning the points at the center. Trim seam allowance points at the center. Press seam allowances to one side.

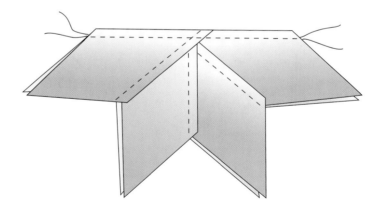

## DESIGNER'S TIP

*Steam-A-Seam 2 is sticky on both sides, so it can be temporarily positioned on both the appliqué and the background fabric. If at first you are not happy with the position, or the appliqué is not smooth and flat, simply peel off the fusible web and reapply it. The bond becomes permanent only after pressing with an iron. Be sure to follow the manufacturer's directions.*

8　Cut a square of fusible web slightly larger than the star. Remove the loose paper. Place the star wrong side down on the fusible web and smooth in place. Cover with the loose paper and fuse with an iron. Remove the loose paper; trim away excess web. Remove the paper backing.

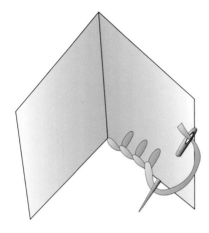

9   Center the star, wrong side down, over the yellow square. Four star points will be centered in the corners of the square; the remaining four points will extend over the sides. Fuse in place, following the manufacturer's directions.

10   Divide the floss into three-thread strands. Stitch around the star using a blanket stitch. Stitch the button to the center.

11   Place the large green backing piece face down; layer the batting and the pieced top, right side up, over the batting. Pin-baste the layers together. Layer and pin-baste the two remaining sets of D rectangles and batting.

12   Quilt around the center square and star points, stitching ¼" (6 mm) from the seams and edges, using yellow thread.

13   Wrap wide bias tape over the short ends of the unit, and stitch in place, encasing the raw edges. Encase the long raw edges of the layered D pieces with wide bias tape.

14   Stitch a zipper to each end of the large piece, lapping the folds of the bias tape to within ⅛" (3 mm) of the zipper teeth. Stitch the other sides of the zippers to the D sections. Then join the D sections by sewing a zipper between them, forming a circle.

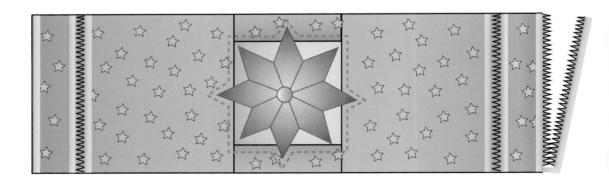

15  Flatten the circle so the star is centered on one side and the middle zipper is centered on the opposite side. Pin together around the edges. Stitch the layers together ⅛" (3 mm) from the raw edges. Trim off the excess ends of the zippers.

16  Stitch a straight yellow line from the quilted star point to the fold on each end of the jewelry roll, dividing the ends into two pockets each. (See photo on page 44. The stitches should not interfere with the zipper.) Then thread the machine with invisible thread. From the inside, stitch across the jewelry roll over the previous stitches on the inner edges of the outer zippers.

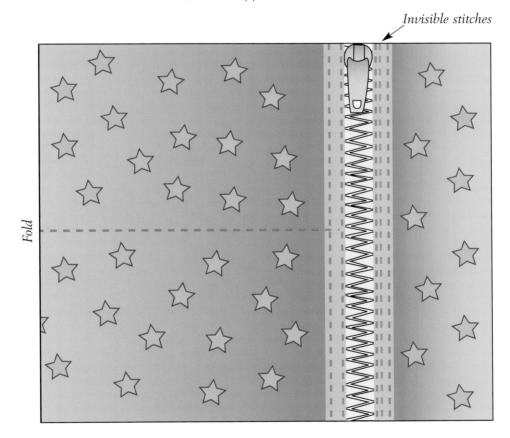

*Invisible stitches*

*Fold*

17  Encase the entire outer edge of the jewelry roll in wide bias tape, mitering the corners.

18  Cut a 1-yd. (0.92 m) length of the narrow bias tape for a tie. Fold the tape in half and knot the ends. Stitch the tie to the underside center of one end of the jewelry roll.

# CRAZY QUILT
## *Photo Frame*

by Denise Bielick

*Crazy quilting* creates a wonderful surface for embroidery and beadwork—skills that Denise learned at an early age from her grandmother. While sifting through her mother's boxes of photos, Denise found this photograph of her grandmother posing in the hollyhocks. Feeling that such a treasured photograph should be displayed instead of hidden away in a box, Denise printed the image on fabric and designed a crazy quilted frame for it. She finished off the frame with embroidered and beaded details.

Photo Frame
8" × 10" (20.5 × 25.5 cm)
*Stitch 'n' flip crazy quilting, photo printing on fabric, embroidery, beadwork*

### MATERIALS

8" × 10" (20.5 × 25.5 cm) mat board

8" × 10" (20.5 × 25.5 cm) mat board with 4½" × 6½" (11.5 × 16.3 cm) oval opening

Two 10" × 12" (25.5 × 30.5 cm) pieces of fabric, one for foundation and one for the frame back

Scraps of a variety of fabrics, cut into straight-sided patches of various shapes and sizes

Scraps of lace, trim, and ribbon

Beads, assorted threads, charms, and buttons

Spray adhesive

Two 8" × 10" (20.5 × 25.5 cm) pieces of quilt batting

Fabric glue

5" × 7" (12.7 × 18 cm) photograph

Computer printer fabric

Computer with photo editing software, scanner, and inkjet color printer

60" (152.5 cm) decorative cording

## Instructions

1   Trace the outer edge and opening of the mat board onto the wrong side of the foundation fabric. Cut out the opening, leaving a 1" (2.5 cm) border. Pin a fabric patch, right side up, in one corner, with edges extending over the outer border.

2   Place a second fabric patch, right side down, over the first one, aligning one edge. Stitch ¼" (6 mm) seam along the aligned edges.

3   Flip the second patch right side up; press along the seamline. Pin in place. Continue to attach patches, working around the frame, until the foundation is covered. For added interest, piece a few patches into a strip and attach the strip as one piece. Secure laces or trims by encasing one edge between layers in a seam.

4   Fold under ¼" (6 mm) seam allowance on the open edge of the last piece, and topstitch it down.

5   Trim the patches even with the edge of the foundation. Trim the opening border to ½" (1.3 cm). Embellish the patchwork with embroidery, charms, and buttons as desired. Instructions for several embroidery stitches can be found on pages 54 and 55.

6   Apply spray adhesive to one side of each mat board. Carefully secure the batting. Trim the batting even with the opening on the front mat board.

7   Place the back fabric piece right side down on the work surface. Place the back mat board, batting down, over the center of the fabric. Working from side to side and top to bottom, wrap the fabric edges over the board edges and glue them down, using fabric glue; pull the fabric taut. Miter fabric at the corners, trimming out some of the fullness.

*Back of mat board*

*Fold at 45-degree angle and glue.*

8   Repeat step 7 for the outer edges of the frame front.
    Clip into the border around the opening every ⅜" (1 cm),
    cutting to within ⅛" (3 mm) of the board. Wrap the clipped
    fabric to the back and glue it down.

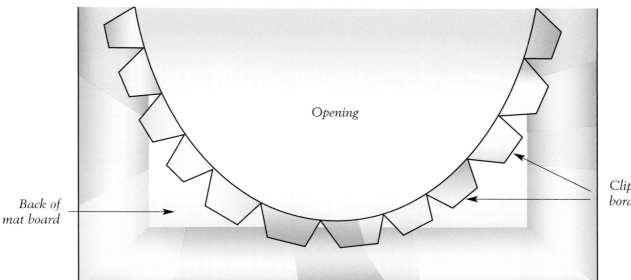

*Opening*

*Back of
mat board*

*Clipped
border*

9   Print the photograph on printable fabric, following the
    manufacturer's directions. Using spray adhesive, attach the
    image to the unfinished side of the back mat board, making
    sure it will be centered in the opening.

10  Glue a ribbon loop to the top center of the unfinished mat
    board back, for hanging the frame.

11  Glue the front to the back, leaving small openings at the
    bottom of the frame and at the bottom of the opening for
    inserting cord ends. Place a book over the frame to weight
    it, and allow it to dry.

12  Glue the cording around the outer edge of the frame,
    inserting the cut ends into the opening at the lower edge.
    Repeat around the edge of the opening.

## Embroidery Stitches

**Bullion Stitch:** Bring the needle and thread to the surface. Insert the needle a short distance away, equal to the desired length of the stitch; bring the needle point back out near the origin. Wrap the thread around the needle, forming a coil the same length as the stitch length. Pull the needle carefully through the coil while holding the coil down on the fabric with your thumb. Pull the thread through the coil until it tightens and insert the needle point back through the fabric at the point where it first appeared. The coil should lie neatly on the surface.

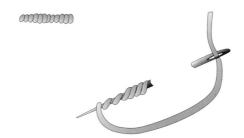

**Bullion Rose:** This is a series of bullion stitches. The first two stitches are side by side in the center. The rest of the stitches curve around these two, slightly overlapping and working outward in a spiral.

**French Knot:** Bring the needle and thread to the surface. Holding the needle parallel to the fabric near the origin, wrap the thread around the needle two or three times. Insert the needle very close to the origin, holding the thread in place close to the wrapped needle. Hold the thread while pulling t he needle through to the underside, releasing the thread as it disappears and forms a soft knot.

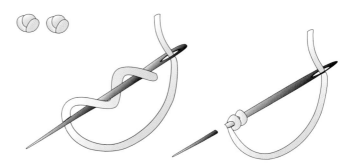

### DESIGNER'S TIP

*There's a trick to embroidering bullion roses, whether with embroidery floss or silk ribbon. To make the bullion stitches curve, you need to make more wraps than the length of the stitch would normally accommodate. The extra wraps of floss or ribbon force the stitch into an arc, which you can then coax to curve in the desired direction.*

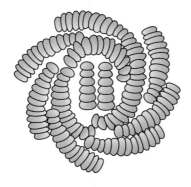

**Feather Stitch:** Bring the needle up at the top of your intended line and pull the ribbon through. Insert the needle a short distance to the left and bring the point out below and half-way between the two points, with the ribbon below the needle. Pull through, forming a V. Repeat, alternating from left to right. Secure the last stitch by inserting the needle just below the last V.

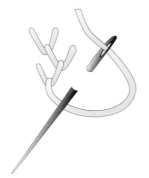
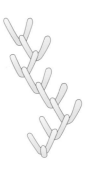

**Lazy Daisy Stitch:** Bring the needle up from the underside at the petal base; insert the needle right next to the origin, and bring the needle back up at the petal tip. Pull the ribbon through the fabric, forming a small, smooth loop. Pass the ribbon over the loop; secure it with a small straight stitch at the tip.

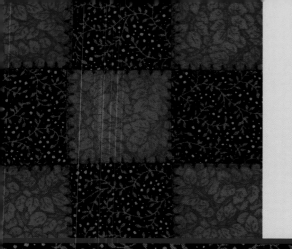

# QUICK-PIECED
## *Checkerboard*

by Janis Bullis

*Alternate light and dark squares* of a checkerboard have always reminded Janis of a simple patchwork quilt design. With rotary cutting and some quick-piecing methods, the game board goes together in a snap. Fabric ties with their ends knotted ingeniously inside miniature wooden flower pots allow you to roll the game board for storage. With the addition of some painted wooden disks for checkers and a matching fabric pouch to carry them, the set makes a clever, thoughtful gift.

Checkerboard
*15^1/2" (39.3 cm) square*
*Quick piecing*

## Instructions

1    Wash, dry, and press all the fabrics. Shrink the batting according to the manufacturer's directions, if desired.

2    Trim the selvages from the fabrics. From the red fabric, cut a 16" (40.5 cm) backing square for the checkerboard. Cut two 5½" × 4½" (14 × 11.5 cm) rectangles and one 5½" × 2½" (14 × 6.5 cm) rectangle for the bag. From the remaining red fabric, cut four 2" × 18" (5 × 46 cm) strips for the checkerboard squares, four 2" × 18" (5 × 46 cm) strips for the borders, and one 1½" × 18" (3.8 × 46 cm) strip for the bag squares.

3    Cut a 5½" × 14½" (14 × 36.8 cm) rectangle of blue fabric for the bag. Then cut enough 2½" (6.5 cm) strips to measure 70" (178 cm) for the binding. Cut four 2" × 18" (5 × 46 cm) strips for the checkerboard squares, three 2" × 18" (5 × 46 cm) strips for the ties, and one 1½" × 18" (3.8 × 46 cm) strip for the bag squares.

## MATERIALS

⅝ yd. (0.6 m) each of two fabrics, one light value and one dark value

½ yd. (0.5 m) square of lightweight cotton quilt batting

Matching threads

24 wooden disks, 1½" (3.8 cm) diameter

Four miniature wooden flower pots with center holes

Acrylic paint in colors to match the fabrics; paintbrush

Clear acrylic sealer or spray varnish

Glue

4   Stitch four 2" (5 cm) strips together, alternating blue and red for the checkerboard squares, using ¼" seams. Press the seam allowances toward the blue strips. Repeat to make a second set.

5   Cut the sets crosswise every 2" (5 cm), cutting 8 four-square units from each set. Stitch the strips of each set back together, alternating colors, aligning the seams, and keeping the seam allowances pressed in opposite directions. Press all the new seam allowances in one direction.

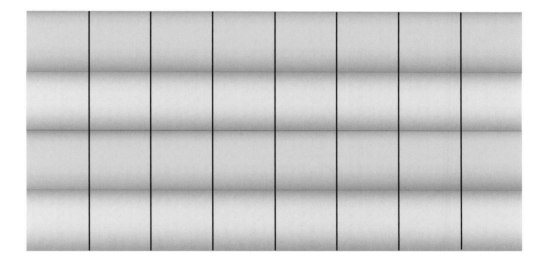

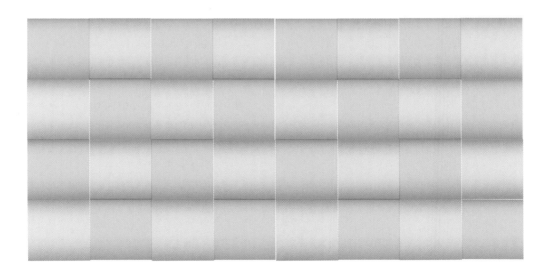

6   Stitch the two sets together along the lengthwise edges to complete the checkerboard.

7   Center a border strip on one side of the checkerboard. Stitch, beginning and ending 1/4" (6 mm) from the corner. Repeat on each side.

8   Fold the checkerboard in half diagonally, corner to corner, so the border strips overlap on the ends; pin. Mark a line from the point where you stopped stitching to the outer edge of the strips, in line with the fold. Stitch. Trim the seam allowances to 1/4" (6 mm) and press open. Repeat at each corner, forming miters.

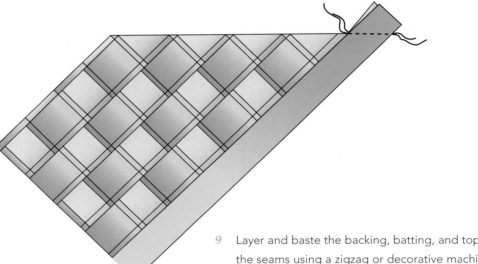

9   Layer and baste the backing, batting, and top. Quilt over the seams using a zigzag or decorative machine stitch.

10  Press the tie strips in half lengthwise. Then refold, aligning the raw edges to the center fold; press. Topstitch along the outer folds.

11  Stitch binding strips together, using diagonal seams. Fold the binding in half lengthwise. Stitch the binding to the outer edge of the borders, mitering the corners (page 94). At the center of one side, catch the ends of the ties in place on the back.

12  Turn the binding to the back and hand-stitch in place.

13  Stitch together the strips for the bag squares; press the seam allowances toward the blue strip. Then cut the strip into ten 1 1/2" (3.8 cm) units. Alternating colors, stitch two sets, each two squares wide and five squares long.

14 Stitch one checkered set to a long edge of the red 5½" × 2½" (14 × 6.5 cm) rectangle; stitch the other set to the opposite edge. Stitch a 5½" × 4½" (14 × 11.5 cm) rectangle to each end of this set.

15 Fold the fabric in half, aligning the squares. Stitch the side seams. Create a "paper-bag" bottom by aligning the side seams to the center bottom and spreading the bottom corner into a triangle. Stitch from fold to fold, 1" (2.5 cm) from the corner, perpendicular to the side seam; you will be stitching close to the seam of the checkered strip.

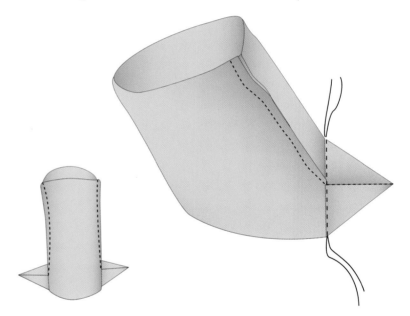

16 Stitch the sides of the blue bag lining, leaving a 3" (7.5 cm) opening along one seam for turning. Create the paper-bag bottom, as in step 15. Slip the lining into the bag, right sides together; stitch the upper edges together. Press the seam toward the lining.

17 Turn the bags right side out through the opening; stitch the opening closed. Turn the lining into the bag and topstitch the upper edge, allowing the lining to extend ¼" (6 mm). Stitch a tie as in step 10. Stitch the center of the tie to the center of the bag back, 2" (5 cm) from the top.

18 Paint twelve red and twelve blue wooden checkers. Paint the flower pots red. Seal all the wooden pieces. Slip the ends of the ties into the flower pot holes; glue in place.

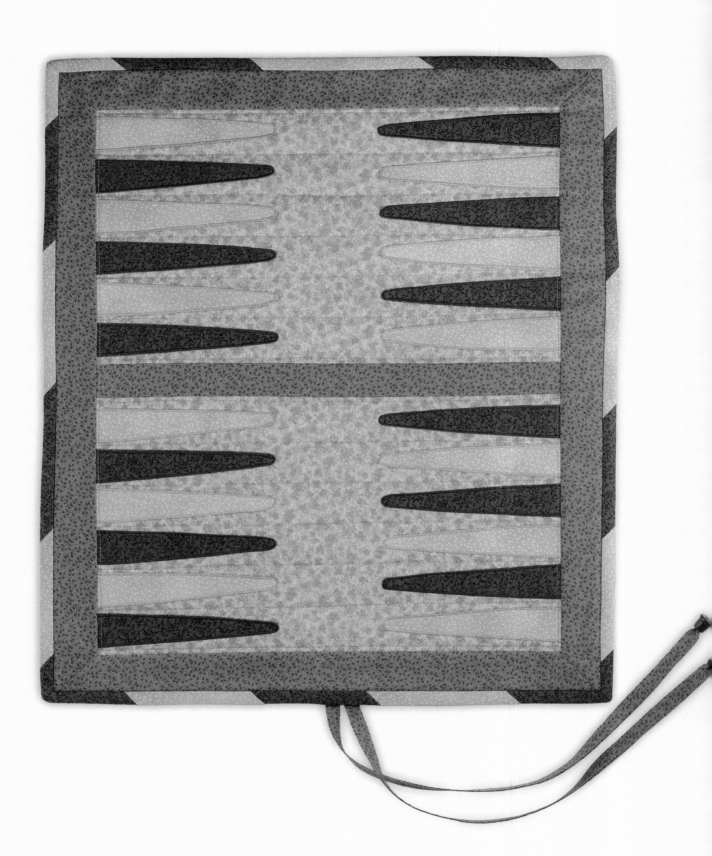

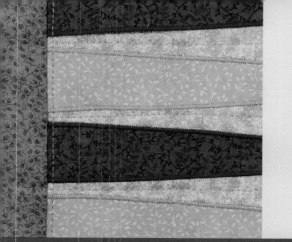

# APPLIQUÉD
# *Backgammon Board*

by Janis Bullis

*Satin stitch appliqué* can create an unlimited number of designs, including many game boards like this backgammon board. As long as the sizes and shapes follow the rules of the game, you can choose any color or print. Board men, doubling cubes, and dice cups can be easily made by painting wooden shapes from the craft store. This game travels easily because Janis designed the board to be rolled up. Matching fabric pouches hold the game pieces and dice.

Backgammon Board
23" × 20" (58.5 × 51 cm)
*Satin stitch appliqué,
channel quilting, pieced binding*

## MATERIALS

**½ yd. (0.5 m) each of light and dark fabrics for spires, binding, and bags**

**¾ yd. (0.7 m) medium-tone fabric for background and backing**

**¼ yd. (0.25 m) medium-tone fabric for border**

**¾ yd. (0.7 m) lightweight batting**

**Scrap white fabric for dice appliqué**

**Lightweight fusible interfacing**

**Paper-backed fusible web**

**Matching threads**

**30 wooden disks, 1" (2.5 cm) diameter**

**6 miniature wooden flower pots for tie ends**

**Wooden cube, ¾" (2 cm) for doubling cube**

**Small adhesive-back numbers**

**Two small wood or cardboard boxes for dice cups**

**Acrylic paints to match the spire colors and background color; paintbrush**

**Spray varnish or sealer**

**Two pair purchased dice**

**Glue**

**Permanent marking pen**

*Spire Pattern*

## Instructions

1   Wash, dry, and press all the fabrics. Shrink the batting according to the manufacturer's directions, if desired.

2   Cut a 25" × 22" (63.5 × 56 cm) rectangle for the backing; set aside. Apply lightweight fusible interfacing to the wrong side of the remaining background fabric. Cut two 9¾" × 16½" (25 × 41.8 cm) rectangles for the game board "tables."

3   Cut two 6½" × 18" (16.3 × 46 cm) rectangles from each of the spire fabrics for the bags. Then cut two 2½" (6.5 cm) strips on the crosswise grain from each of the remaining pieces for the binding. Set these aside.

4   Apply lightweight fusible interfacing to the wrong side of the remaining spire fabrics. Then fuse paper-backed fusible web to each fabric. Trace the spire pattern onto the paper backing of each piece twelve times. Cut out the spires.

5   Remove the paper backing from the spires. Arrange the spires on the tables, following the diagram, opposite. Fuse the spires in place. Satin stitch around the sides and curved ends of each spire.

6   Cut two 2" × 23¾" (5 × 60.3 cm) strips from the crosswise grain of the border fabric for the top and bottom borders. Cut two 2" × 20" (5 × 51 cm) strips for the side borders. Cut two 2" × 36" (5 × 91.5 cm) strips for the bag ties. Cut the center bar 16½" × 1¾" (41.8 × 4.5 cm); back it with lightweight fusible interfacing.

7   Join the tables with the center bar, using ¼" (6 mm) seam allowances. Apply the border strips as in steps 7 and 8 on page 60. Layer and baste the backing, batting, and quilt top. Outline-quilt around the outer edge of the board just inside the borders and along the edges of the center bar. Then channel stitch between the spires.

8   Make the ties as on page 60, step 10. Mark the binding strips every 5½" (14 cm) along one edge. Cut at the marks at 45-degree angle. Join the strips, alternating colors. Apply the binding as on page 60, steps 11 and 12.

9   Apply lightweight fusible interfacing to the back of the white fabric. Then fuse paper-backed fusible web to the fabric.

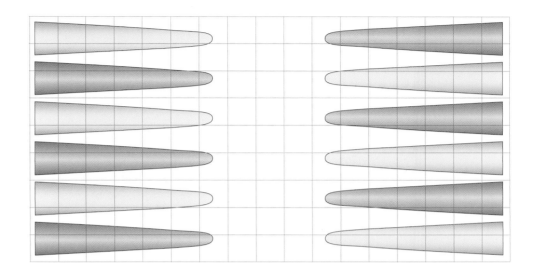

*1 square = 1" (2.5 cm)*

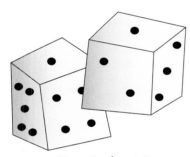

*Dice Appliqué Pattern*

Trace the dice pattern onto the paper backing; cut out. Fuse the dice to the outer bag fabric, with the bottom edge about 3" (7.5 cm) above the center of the strip. Satin stitch around the dice. Add dots with a permanent marker.

10  Finish the bag, following steps 15 to 17 on page 61; disregard reference to checkered strips. Make a second bag, using alternate colors for the outer bag and lining.

11  Paint 15 dark and 15 light wooden game disks; paint four dark and two light wooden flower pots. Paint the dice cups in colors to match the game pieces. Paint the doubling cube the same color as the background fabric. Seal all the wood pieces.

12  Slip the ends of the ties into the flower pot holes; glue in place. Adhere the numbers 2 and 4 to opposite sides of the doubling cube; then 8 and 16 to opposite sides, and 32 and 64 to the remaining two sides. Play backgammon!

## DESIGNER'S TIP

*Lightweight fusible interfacing gives appliqué and background fabrics a little extra body and makes the appliqué process a little easier. You can probably do the satin stitching without additional tear-away stabilizer. It also adds a bit more stiffness, which is a desirable thing in a project like this game board.*

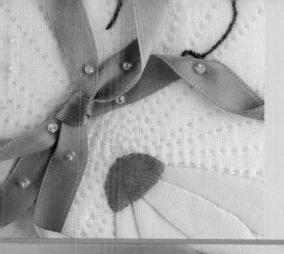

# VINTAGE
# *Hankie Pillow*

by Barbara Boyd

*A mother planning her daughter's wedding* asked Barbara to turn some family heirloom handkerchiefs and lace into two ring bearer pillows. Eagerly accepting the challenge, Barbara designed and created delicate pillows with hand-appliquéd and embroidered flowers, hand quilting, and beadwork. Finding the materials inspiring, Barbara continues to create one-of-a-kind pillows from vintage handkerchiefs. The appliqué pieces are cut from hankies in various colors. She uses crocheted edgings for leaves and other accents. Each pillow is an original design that evolves from the colors and materials of the hankies.

Pillow
*12" (30.5 cm) square*
*Hand quilting, hand appliqué,*
*embroidery, beadwork*

## MATERIALS

½ yd. (0.5 m) white cotton fabric

Lightweight polyester or cotton batting

Vintage handkerchief with lace edging for background; size will determine finished pillow size

Fabric marking pencil

Neutral quilting thread

Between needles, size 10 or 12, for hand quilting

Small quilting hoop

Vintage handkerchiefs in assorted colors for appliqués

Lightweight, nonwoven, fusible interfacing

Freezer paper

Fine silk threads to match appliqués

Straw needles, size 10 or 12, for hand-appliqué

Green crochet edging cut from a handkerchief

Embroidery floss in desired color for pansy face

Green embroidery floss for stems and vines

Seed beads for baby's breath

½ yd. (0.5 m) double-sided satin ribbon, ⅜" (9 mm) wide

Pillow form or fiberfill

## Instructions

1   Wash, dry, and press all the fabrics. Shrink the batting according to the manufacturer's directions, if desired.

2   Mark points about 1" (2.5 cm) apart along the sides of the handkerchief center. Also mark a dot 4" (10 cm) diagonally from the lower right corner. Then mark quilting lines from the outer points to the dot.

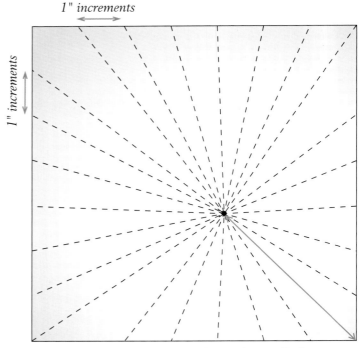

*1" increments*

*1" increments*

*Mark dot 4" diagonally from corner*

## DESIGNER'S TIP

*Group colored hankies according to their color families. When you create a layered appliqué, such as the pansy or rose, use pieces from two or three hankies. The different color values, tints, and tones give dimension to the appliqué. Also, the slightly different surfaces of the hankies, due to variations in fiber content and thread count, add visual texture. Simply cutting the appliqué pieces with grainlines running in different directions creates interest.*

3　Cut two cotton squares for the pillow front and back 2" (5 cm) larger than the hankie, including lace edging. Set the back aside. Cut batting the same size as the pillow front. Center the hankie on the pillow front, right sides up; layer them over the batting. Baste.

4　Hand-quilt the marked design.

5　Trace the appliqué designs onto the dull side of freezer paper; number the pieces. Cut out the patterns.

6　Fuse interfacing to the wrong side of the colored hankies to be used for appliqué pieces. Place the patterns, shiny side down, onto the right side of the desired hankies. Press with an iron to temporarily "fuse" them in place. Trace around the pieces, using a fabric marking pencil; mark dotted lines where pieces will be overlapped by other pieces. Cut them out, allowing 3/16" (4.5 mm) allowance around each for turning under.

7　Remove the freezer paper. Arrange the pieces of the rose on the quilted handkerchief, beginning with #1 and overlapping consecutive pieces; pin in place. Use the photo on page 66 for placement.

8　Thread a straw needle with 18" (46 cm) length of fine silk thread to match the rose fabrics. Beginning with section #1, use the tip of the needle to turn under the fabric edge up to the marked line. Take small invisible stitches to secure the appliqué. Do not stitch the underlapping edge. Stitch each piece in turn.

9    Cut a 1¼" (3.2 cm) square of fabric for the rose bud. Fold in half diagonally, wrong sides together. Fold each point down about ¼" (6 mm) from the center point. Baste and gather the lower edge; trim off excess fabric. Stitch the bud near the rose. Gather a piece of crocheted edging cut from another hankie, and tack over the base of the bud.

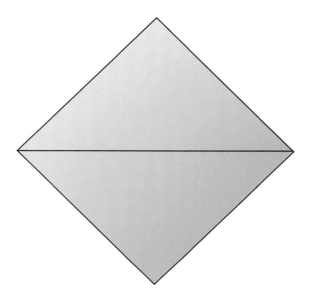

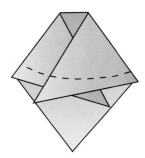

10    Follow step 8 for the pansy. Cut a piece of crocheted trim from a hankie; gather to form a leaf. Slip the leaf under the edge before stitching section 3 in place.

11    Follow step 8 for the tulip and the daisy.

12    Embroider straight-stitch lines for the pansy face, using two strands of coordinating embroidery floss. With a stem stitch, embroider free-form stems and vines, using two strands of green embroidery floss.

13    Tie the ribbon in a bow; if using the pillow for a ring bearer, tie trinket rings into the center of the bow. Secure the ribbon to the pillow front, attaching a seed bead with each stitch. Twist the ribbon as you go to give it a floating appearance.

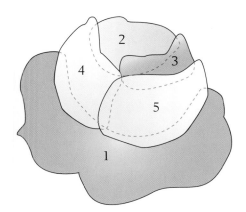

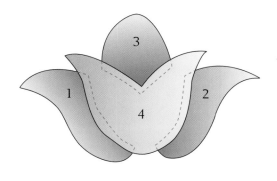

*Appliqué Patterns*

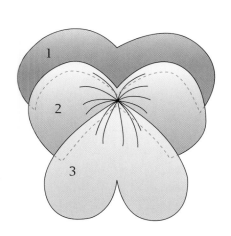

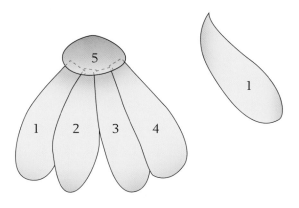

**14** Stitch seed beads in random clusters between the flowers to resemble baby's breath. Stitch seed beads to the lace edging here and there to secure it to the pillow front.

**15** Pin the pillow front and back right sides together. Stitch the ½" (1.3 cm) seam, leaving an opening for turning. Turn right side out.

**16** Insert a pillow form or fiberfill. Stitch the opening closed.

# FOILED
# *Velvet Pillow*

by Laura Murray

*Complex designs* with rich textures are inspiring for Laura. Her designs incorporate products and techniques that have lots of creative possibilities. She experimented with foiling on rich velvet with exciting results. She also wanted to use D'UVA® powders, a relatively new product that tints fabrics in interesting ways. She applied the powders to shiny white acetate and produced a rich background for the foiled velvet squares. D'UVA products are very easy to use and are more forgiving than other paints and dyes. The pillow is hand-washable; but do not dry-clean it because the cleaning solvents will remove the foil.

Pillow
*20" (51 cm) square*
*Foiled velvet, coloring with D'UVA powders,*
*free-motion quilting*

## MATERIALS

2/3 yd. (0.63 m) white or cream satin, silk charmeuse, or synthetic fabric with a shiny surface

D'UVA ChromaCoal™ Powder in desired colors

2" (5 cm) bristle brush

Kneadable eraser

Kitchen parchment paper

Iron or heat gun

2/3 yd. (0.63 m) black or dark red washable velvet

Rubber stamp, 5" (12.7 cm) square (the one used was designed by Sandi Obertin)

Water-soluble textile adhesive

2" (5 cm) foam brush

Foil in gold, silver, aqua, and red

Needle board for pressing velvet

Fusible adhesive web

18" (46 cm) square lightweight batting

18" (46 cm) square fabric for backing

Gold metallic thread

Rotary cutter, mat, and ruler

2 3/8 yd. (2.2 m) black fringe

1 yd. (0.92 m) fusible knit interfacing

20" (51 cm) pillow form

## DESIGNER'S TIP

*D'UVA powders are transparent, which means they will interact with the color of the background fabric. For instance, if you apply yellow powder to blue fabric, the result will be green. They do not not show on dark background colors. Applied to white fabric, the colors will be truer, brighter. A slightly creamy background will tone them down and warm them up just a bit.*

## Instructions

1   Mark out an 18" (46 cm) square on the satin background fabric. Using a bristle brush, apply various colors of D'UVA ChromaCoal powders over the surface until you are pleased with the blending effect. If you make a mistake, simply erase the color, using a kneadable eraser.

2   Cover the fabric with a sheet of kitchen parchment paper. Heat set the color into the fabric, using an iron and following the manufacturer's instructions. Keep the iron moving to prevent imprinting the steam vents into the design. Alternatively, omit the parchment paper and use a heat gun (intended for crafting), applying heat directly to the fabric. Keep the heat gun moving slowly just above the fabric surface. Once they have been heat set, the colors are permanent.

3  Paint textile adhesive onto the rubber stamp, using a foam brush; stamp the velvet. Repeat three times, leaving some space between the images. Allow to dry for several hours.

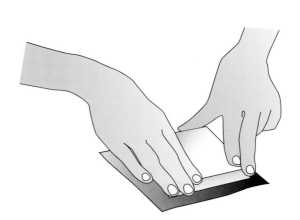

4  Place gold foil, color side up, over the stamped image and rub with the edge of a dry iron on cotton setting. Repeat with the silver, aqua, and red foils to achieve multiple colors in the design.

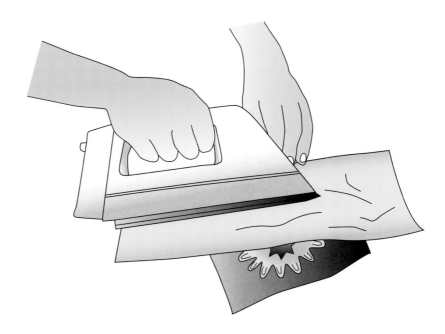

## DESIGNER'S TIP

*A backing fabric with a distinct printed image can become the template for the quilted design. Wind the decorative thread onto the bobbin. Then, with the backing facing up, free-motion quilt, following the printed design.*

5   Place the velvet face down over the needle board. Apply fusible adhesive web onto the wrong side of the velvet. Cut out the image squares, and remove the paper backing.

6   Place the velvet squares, evenly spaced, on the background fabric. Place parchment paper over the images to protect them. Fuse in place. Using black thread, zigzag around the edges of the squares.

7   Layer the front over the batting and backing. Baste. Quilt as desired, using the gold metallic thread. Cut the pillow front to 18" (46 cm).

8   Cut 2" (5 cm) strips of velvet. Hand-baste them to the sides of the pillow front. Stitch ¼" (6 mm) seams, beginning and ending ¼" (6 mm) from the corners.

9   Fold the pillow front in half diagonally, so the border strips overlap on the ends; pin. Mark a line from the point where you stopped stitching to the outer edge of the strips, in line with the fold. Stitch. Trim the seam allowances to ¼" (6 mm) and finger-press open. Repeat at each corner, forming miters.

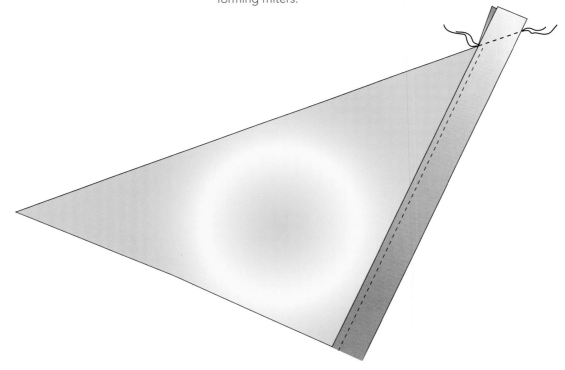

10  Hand-baste fringe to the outer edges on the right side of the pillow front.

11  Cut two pieces of velvet 20" × 14" (51 × 35.5 cm) for the pillow back. Place the velvet face down over a needle board. Apply fusible knit interfacing to the wrong side of each piece to help stabilize the velvet.

12  Turn under and stitch a narrow single-fold hem on one long edge of each back piece. Pin the pieces, right sides together to the pillow front, overlapping the hemmed edges. Hand-baste around the outer edge. Stitch ¼" (6 mm) seam, taking care not to catch the fringe in the stitches.

13  Turn the pillow cover right side out. Pull the fringe gently to coax the seam out to the edge. Insert the pillow form into the lapped opening.

## ALTERNATIVE METHOD FOR FOILING

This method works well for foiling simple shapes. It doesn't require drying time, like the liquid adhesive method used in the steps on page 75.

1  Trace or draw the desired designs onto the paper backing of paper-backed fusible adhesive web. If your designs are not symmetrical, trace their mirror images. Cut them out.

2  Place the designs, adhesive side down, over the fabric. Fuse in place, following the manufacturer's directions. Allow to cool. Remove the paper backing.

3  Apply the foil, following step 4 on page 75.

# ABSTRACT
# *Appliqué Pillow*

by Julann Windsperger

*Design inspiration* can come from any source at any time; you just have to keep your eyes and mind open. Julann adapted the abstract design for this pillow from some interesting doodles printed on a paper coffee cup. She used synthetic fleece for the fusible appliqués to create surface texture and loft. Besides being easy to work with, fleece also offers lots of color choices and makes a bold statement when outlined with the black bias tape.

Pillow
*20" (51 cm) square*
*Appliqué with bias strips*

## MATERIALS

**1¼ yd. (1.15 m) upholstery fabric**

**Synthetic fleece scraps or ¼ yd. (0.25 m) each of various colors**

**One roll black fusible bias tape, ¼" (6 mm) wide**

**Mini Iron®**

**Iron; press cloth**

**Two 22" (56 cm) squares of Armo Press Soft for backing**

**2½ yd. (2.3 m) narrow upholstery cording**

**Paper-backed fusible adhesive web**

**Two 22" (56 cm) squares of batting**

**Thread: black, color to match main fabric, and variegated**

## Instructions

1   Measure the cording circumference and add 1" (2.5 cm) to determine the width of the bias strips needed for covering the cord. Cut 2½ yd. (2.3 m) of bias strips with this width. Also cut two 21" (53.5 cm) squares for the pillow front and back.

2   Enlarge the design or draw your own abstract design. Trace the mirror image of each appliqué section onto the paper backing of the fusible web. (If using your own design, trace mirror images of each shape.) Cut out the shapes. Fuse them to the wrong side of the fleece, using a press cloth. Cut out the fleece shapes.

3   Remove the paper backing. Arrange the shapes on the pillow front, butting edges that will be crossed by the bias tape. Allow outer edges of the corner circular shape to extend beyond the seamline. Fuse in place, using a press cloth.

4   Fuse black bias tape around the design shapes, using the Mini Iron and following the pattern or your own design. Turn under ends; miter corners and points. Ease to fit around tight curves.

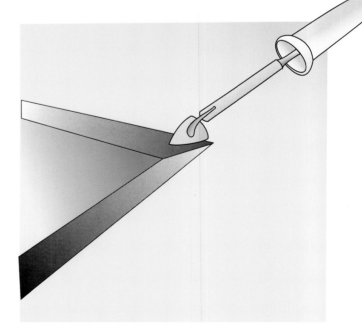

5   Layer the pillow front over the batting and backing; pin-baste. Stitch along both outer edges of the bias tape, using black thread. Work on one design area at a time. If the bias tape loosens, fuse with the Mini Iron again.

6   Apply bias tape designs in open areas as desired, turning under or hiding ends under overlapping strips.

7   Cover the cording with the bias fabric strip, using a zipper foot or cording foot. Apply the cording to the outer edge of the pillow front, clipping the cording seam allowances at the corners. Where the ends meet, join the strip ends with a diagonal seam to reduce bulk; cut the cording so the ends just meet.

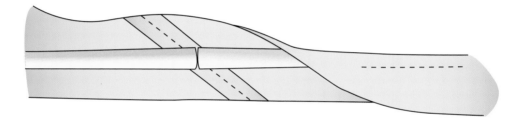

8   Layer and pin-baste the pillow back, batting, and backing. Using variegated thread, quilt freehand in any desired pattern. Recut the outer edge to square up the pillow back.

9   Pin the pillow front to the back, right sides together. Stitching from the wrong side of the pillow front, stitch all four corners and three sides, just inside the stitching line for the cording; leave a 16" (40.5 cm) opening on the fourth side for inserting the pillow form.

10  Turn the pillow right side out. Pull the cording to the outer edge all around the pillow. Insert the pillow form. Hand-stitch the opening closed.

## DESIGNER'S TIP

*Normally you should try to avoid pressing fleece when you are using it for a garment because pressing destroys its loft. For appliqué, however, less loft is a good thing. The key to creating a compact, smooth surface is using a press cloth. I use a large piece of muslin and I keep the iron moving to prevent imprinting steam holes in the fleece.*

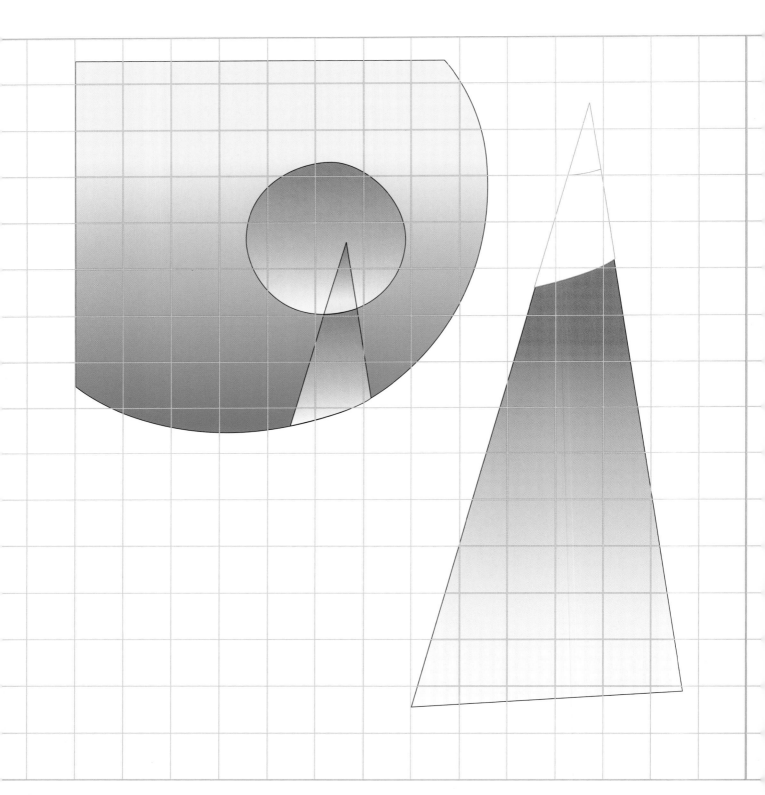

*Abstract Pillow Patterns*

*1 square = 1" (2.5 cm)*

# POINSETTIA
## *Table Topper*

by Denise Bielick

*This holiday table topper* is an example of what can happen when technology is combined with traditional quilting methods. Denise's embroidery machine created the intricate cardinal pictures at the touch of her finger. Then she made the rest of the quilt with conventional piecing. Denise adapted the Carolina Lily pattern, which has always reminded her of a poinsettia, to frame the embroidered squares in each corner. The method requires some set-in seaming, which is a little trickier than standard block piecing, but the results are worth the extra effort.

Table Topper
*36" (91.5 cm) square*
*Digital machine embroidery,*
*conventional piecing,*
*set-in-seam piecing, template*
*and stitch-in-the-ditch quilting*

## MATERIALS

**1 yd. (0.92 m) ecru background fabric**

**⅔ yd. (0.63 m) red fabric**

**1 yd. (0.92 m) backing fabric**

**36" (91.5 cm) square of lightweight batting**

**⅓ yd. (0.32 m) green fabric for binding**

**Machine embroidery design to fit 6" (15 cm) square. Design used is #CH042 from Stitchitize Embroidery Design Service, enlarged to 4½" (11.5 cm) tall**

**Embroidery threads, needles, stabilizer**

**Threads, including red quilting thread**

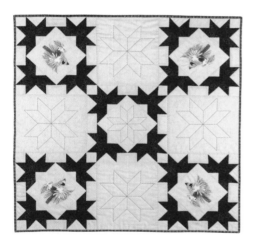

## Instructions

1   Wash, dry, and press all the fabrics. Shrink the batting according to the manufacturer's directions, if desired.

2   Machine-embroider your chosen design on four 10" (25.5 cm) squares of ecru fabric. Cut the squares to 6½" (16.3 cm). Cut a plain 6½" (16.3 cm) square of ecru fabric for the center. These will be referred to as A.

3   Cut the following from the ecru fabric: one 10½" (26.7 cm) strip, cut into four 9" (23 cm) rectangles (B); one 4⅛" (10.4 cm) strip, cut into ten 4⅛" (10.4 cm) squares, then cut diagonally into four triangles each (C); one 3⅜" (8.5 cm) strip, cut into twenty 1⅞" (4.7 cm) rectangles (D); one 2¼" (6 cm) strip, cut into ten 2¼" (6 cm) squares (E); and one 1⅞" (4.7 cm) strip, cut into sixteen 1⅞" (4.7 cm) squares (F).

4   Cut seven 1½" (3.8 cm) strips from the red fabric. Using the templates, cut sixty (G) diamonds and sixty (H) diamonds. To avoid confusion later, mark an H on the wrong side of the H pieces, using chalk pencil.

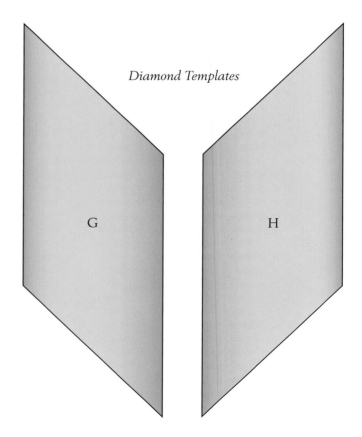

*Diamond Templates*

G

H

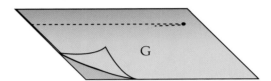

5   Place a G diamond and an H diamond right sides together. Stitch as shown, stopping ¼" (6 mm) from the edge. Backstitch two stitches to secure. Repeat to join all sixty units. Press the seam allowances toward the G pieces.

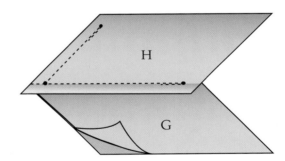

### DESIGNER'S TIP

*When using the set-in-seaming method, take the time to mark dots on the wrong sides of the pieces, ¼" (6 mm) from the ends. Pin the pieces in place, matching up the dots. Stitch one side at a time, backstitching two or three stitches at the dots to secure. Then cut the thread, pin the next side in place, reposition the fabric under the presser foot, and stitch the adjacent seam in the same way. Keep all of the seam allowances turned out of the way to make stitching easy.*

6   Stitch two units, right sides together, beginning at the seam on the pointed end and stopping ¼" (6 mm) from the edge; backstitch. Don't catch the seam allowances in the stitches. Repeat to make twenty sets.

7   Stitch an E triangle to the short side of each of the remaining twenty units. Press the seam allowances away from the triangles. (It is helpful to arrange the pieces on the work surface to avoid stitching the triangle to the wrong edge.)

8    Stitch a set from step 6 to a set from step 7, aligning the seams at the center. Stitch to the edge on the end with the triangle; stop stitching ¼" (6 mm) from the other edge. Press the seam allowances away from the triangle.

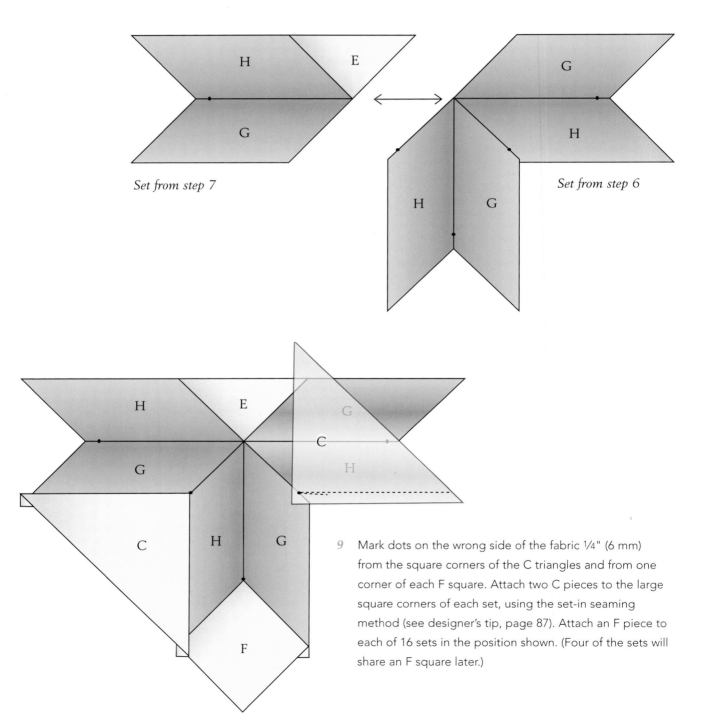

*Set from step 7*

*Set from step 6*

9    Mark dots on the wrong side of the fabric ¼" (6 mm) from the square corners of the C triangles and from one corner of each F square. Attach two C pieces to the large square corners of each set, using the set-in seaming method (see designer's tip, page 87). Attach an F piece to each of 16 sets in the position shown. (Four of the sets will share an F square later.)

10  Sew the sets with F squares to the four sides of each of the embroidered squares. Sew the sets without F squares to the four sides of the plain A square. Press seam allowances away from the center.

11  Set-in-seam the D rectangles to the open spaces of each block.

12  Sew the 9" (23 cm) sides of the B rectangles to the center (plain) set. Set-in-seam an embroidered block to each corner of the center set, taking care to position the embroidered designs with the bottoms at each outer corner.

13  Mark the plain squares using the quilting templates; copy and repeat. Layer and baste the backing, batting, and quilt top. Stitch in the ditch around the blocks and "poinsettias." Quilt the designs using red thread.

14  Bind the quilt as desired.

*Quilting Templates*

# SNOWFLAKE
# *Appliqué Table Mat*

by Patricia Converse

*Hawaiian appliqué quilting* is perfect for creating
snowflakes, even if the geography seems odd. Hawaiian
appliqué quilts often have identical quadrants made by
folding the fabric before cutting the shapes. For a wintery
table mat, Patricia created snowflake designs in much
the same way, folding the fabric before transferring the
cutting lines to create a crystal with six identical arms.
She used blue and white fabrics and shimmering metallic
threads for a crisp winter feeling.

Table Mat
*17" (43 cm) diameter*
*Satin-stitch appliqué*

## MATERIALS

**Four 18" × 22" (46 × 56 cm)
fat quarters: one white, one
background, one backing,
one binding.**

**Scrap fabric for highlights**

**Thin cotton batting,
18" (46 cm) square**

**Lightweight nonwoven fusible
interfacing, 18" (46 cm) square**

**11" × 17" (28 × 43 cm) paper
for tracing pattern**

**Masking tape; pencil**

**Small, sharp-pointed scissors**

**Tear-away stabilizer**

**Cotton threads: white, black,
and background color**

**White rayon thread**

**Silver metallic thread**

## Instructions

1    Wash, dry, and press all the fabrics. Soak interfacing in hot
     tap water for five minutes and air-dry. Shrink the batting
     according to the manufacturer's directions, if desired.

2    Cut an 18" (46 cm) square of white fabric. Fuse the
     interfacing to the wrong side of the fabric, following the
     manufacturer's directions.

3    Trace the pattern onto the upper half of 11" × 17" (28 ×
     43 cm) paper; include the cutting lines, vertical base line,
     horizontal base line, outer cutting line, and basting lines.
     Fold the paper in half on the horizontal base line, wrong
     sides together, and trace the lower half of the pattern, using
     a window or light box, if necessary. The pattern will be for
     half a snowflake.

4    Fold the white fabric in half, with the interfacing on the
     outside; finger-press along the fold. Unfold the fabric, and
     tape it face down over the pattern, aligning the fold line of
     the fabric to the vertical base line of the pattern. Using a
     sharp pencil, trace all the lines onto the interfacing. It may
     be easier to mark the points with dots and then connect
     them using a straightedge.

## DESIGNER'S TIP

*Test your satin stitch settings and practice stitching on cutout shapes and openings similar to the ones in the snowflake. Set the machine to stitch a very close zigzag, a scant 1/8" (3 mm) wide. Stitches should lie close enough together to hide the raw edge but they should not pile up on each other. Use an open-toe embroidery foot or appliqué foot. Begin along one side of a shape. To make neat corners, leave the needle down in the fabric at the outside of the corner, raise the presser foot, pivot, lower the presser foot, and continue. Stop when stitches just meet. Pull the thread tails to the back and knot before trimming.*

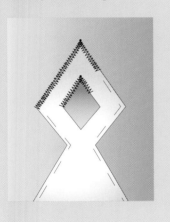

5   Fold the fabric right sides together along the vertical base line. Machine-baste the layers together only along the basting lines to hold them together for cutting.

6   Cut out the snowflake, using very sharp small to medium-size scissors, and cutting both layers at once. The areas that are basted will be cut away. Open the snowflake. Press gingerly if necessary.

7   Cut the background fabric 18" (46 cm) square. Mark the right side center with a pin. Center the snowflake, right side up, on the right side of the background fabric. Cut pieces of accent fabric slightly larger than the center star and cutouts of the points. Slip the pieces in place under the openings. Pin tear-away stabilizer to the underside of the layers.

8   Machine-baste the snowflake to the background, using white cotton thread and stitching very near the cut edges. These stitches will be hidden by the satin stitches.

9   Satin stitch over all the cut edges, using white rayon thread. Pivot at the corners (see the designer's tip). Pull all the thread tails to the back; tie with a square knot and trim. Carefully remove the stabilizer. Press lightly.

10   Cut the backing fabric 18" (46 cm) square. Layer and baste the backing, batting, and quilt top. If using safety pins, avoid pinning directly on the snowflake.

11   Quilt the mat, using metallic thread and following lines of the pattern. Begin by quilting through the six radials. Then quilt the remaining lines working from the center outward. Quilt continuously whenever possible. Pull all thread tails to the back and tie. Bury the thread tails and knots between layers of the quilt.

12   Align the pattern to the snowflake and mark the outer cutting line. Baste 1/4" (6 mm) inside the cutting line. Using a rotary cutter and straightedge, cut on the cutting line.

13   Cut three binding strips 1³/4" × 21" (4.5 × 53.5 cm). Join strips with diagonal seams to minimize bulk; trim seam allowances to 1/4" (6 mm) and press open. Fold strip in half lengthwise and press.

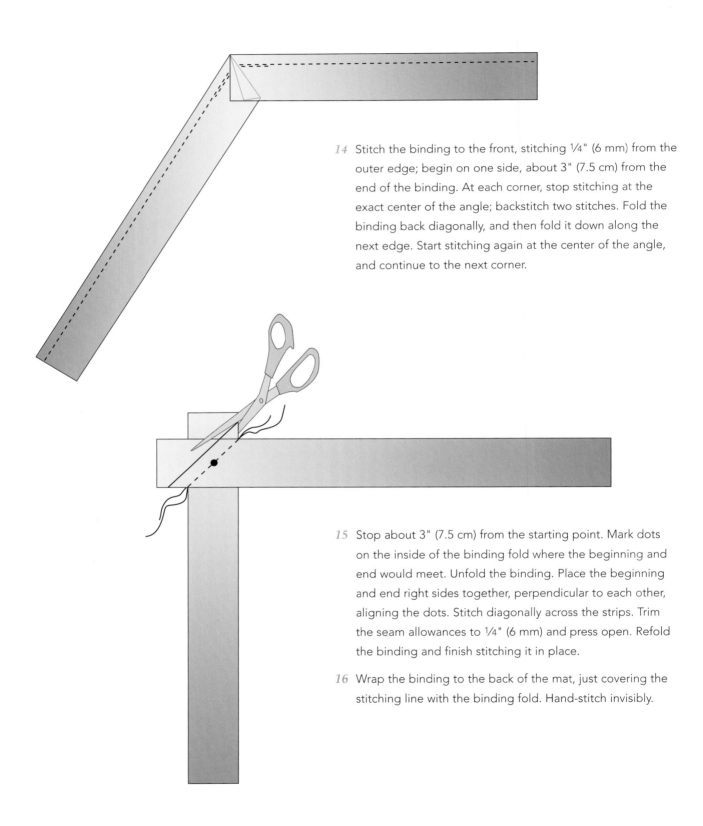

14  Stitch the binding to the front, stitching ¼" (6 mm) from the outer edge; begin on one side, about 3" (7.5 cm) from the end of the binding. At each corner, stop stitching at the exact center of the angle; backstitch two stitches. Fold the binding back diagonally, and then fold it down along the next edge. Start stitching again at the center of the angle, and continue to the next corner.

15  Stop about 3" (7.5 cm) from the starting point. Mark dots on the inside of the binding fold where the beginning and end would meet. Unfold the binding. Place the beginning and end right sides together, perpendicular to each other, aligning the dots. Stitch diagonally across the strips. Trim the seam allowances to ¼" (6 mm) and press open. Refold the binding and finish stitching it in place.

16  Wrap the binding to the back of the mat, just covering the stitching line with the binding fold. Hand-stitch invisibly.

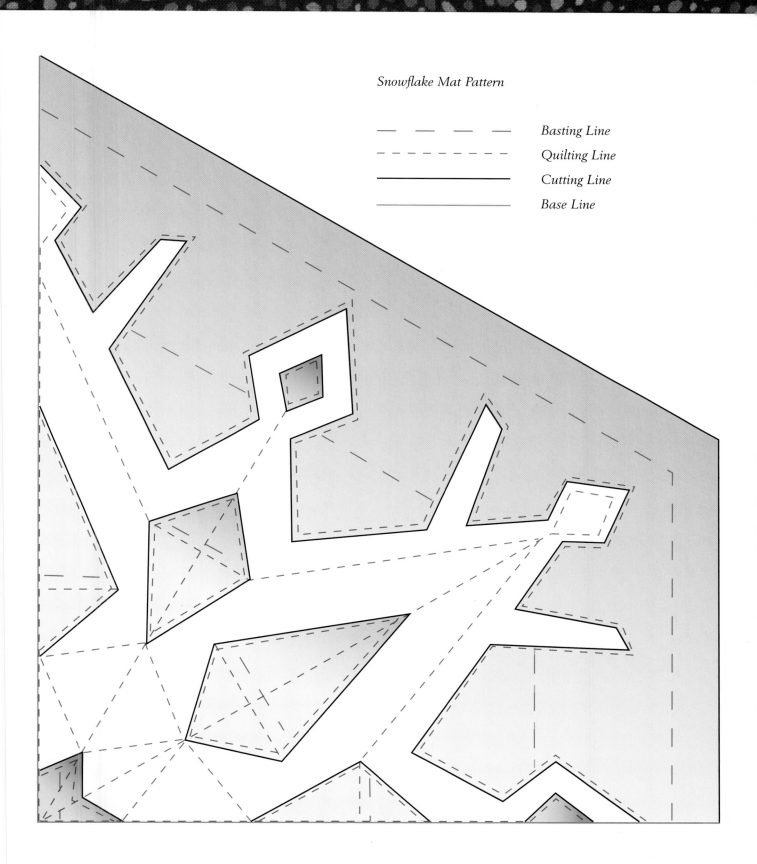

Snowflake Mat Pattern

— — — — —   *Basting Line*

- - - - - -   *Quilting Line*

——————   *Cutting Line*

——————   *Base Line*

# SEASONAL
## *Table Mat Set*

by Janis Bullis

*Placemats and table runners* with seasonal colors and appliqués can quickly transform your dining table as summer turns to fall, or winter to spring. Janis's designs have center panels and corner blocks that showcase the appliqués. This fall set uses rich autumn colors and appliqués of oak leaves, acorns, and pumpkins. For winter, you might use holly leaves, berries, and poinsettias. In the spring, create a new look with pastel tulips, butterflies, and strawberries. Transition into summer with bold sunflowers, bluebirds, and bumblebees. Experiment with your own designs and color schemes.

Table Runner and Placemats
*15" × 48" (38 × 122 cm)*
*11" × 17" (28 × 43 cm)*
*Satin stitch appliqué*

## MATERIALS

**Four or five coordinating fabrics in colors suitable for the season**

**Nonwoven lightweight fusible interfacing**

**Paper-backed fusible web**

**Lightweight quilt batting**

**Matching threads**

## *Table Runner Instructions*

1   Wash, dry, and press all the fabrics. Shrink the batting according to the manufacturer's directions, if desired.

2   Cut the center panel 8½" × 41½" (21.8 × 105.5 cm). Cut two long sashing strips 1" × 41½" (2.5 × 105.5 cm); cut two short sashing strips 1" × 9½" (2.5 × 24.3 cm). Cut four 3½" (9 cm) corner squares for the border corner stones. Then cut several 3⅞" (9.7 cm) squares of each of the fabrics for the triangle-squares that make up the border; cut them in half diagonally.

3   Apply fusible web to the wrong side of the appliqué fabrics. Trace the desired shapes and cut them out. Fuse a medium-size shape to each corner square. Fuse the large and small shapes in a scattered arrangement over the center panel. Satin stitch the outer edges of all the appliqués, using matching thread.

4   Stitch the long sashing strips to the outer edges of the center panel; press the seam allowances toward the sashing. Stitch the shorter sashing strips to the ends of the panel.

5   Stitch triangle-squares together along the long bias edge; press seam allowances toward the darker fabric. Stitch 14 triangle-squares together for each side border; sew the side borders to the center panel. Stitch three triangle squares together for the end borders; add an appliquéd corner square to each end of both borders. Stitch the end borders to the panel, aligning seam intersections at the corners.

6   Cut quilt batting and backing about 18" × 50" (46 × 127 cm). Layer, baste, and quilt the runner as desired.

7   Cut binding strips 2½" (6.5 cm) wide. Bind the table runner.

## *Placemat Instructions*

1   Cut the center panel 7" × 10" (18 × 25.5 cm). Cut two long sashing strips 1" × 10" (2.5 × 25.5 cm); cut two short sashing strips 1" × 8" (2.5 × 20.5 cm). Cut four 3½" (9 cm) squares for the border corner stones. Then cut several 2⅜" (6.2 cm) squares of each of the fabrics for the triangle-squares that make up the border; cut them in half diagonally.

## DESIGNER'S TIP

*Before you select fabrics for your seasonal placemats and table runner, draw the designs on graph paper and experiment with different color combinations for the triangle-squares along the outer borders. When you find an arrangement you like, you will have a better idea of how much fabric to buy and how many squares to cut of each color. Then the drawing will help you assemble them in the right order.*

2   Follow steps 3 to 4 opposite. Stitch triangle-squares together along the long bias edge; press seam allowances toward the darker fabric. Stitch seven triangle squares together for the top and bottom borders; stitch them to the panel. Stitch six triangle-squares together in two rows for each side border; add an appliquéd corner square to each end of both borders. Sew the side borders to the center panel.

3   Cut quilt batting and backing about 13" × 19" (33 × 48.5 cm). Layer, baste, and quilt the placemats as desired.

4   Cut binding strips 2½" (6.5 cm) wide. Bind the placemats.

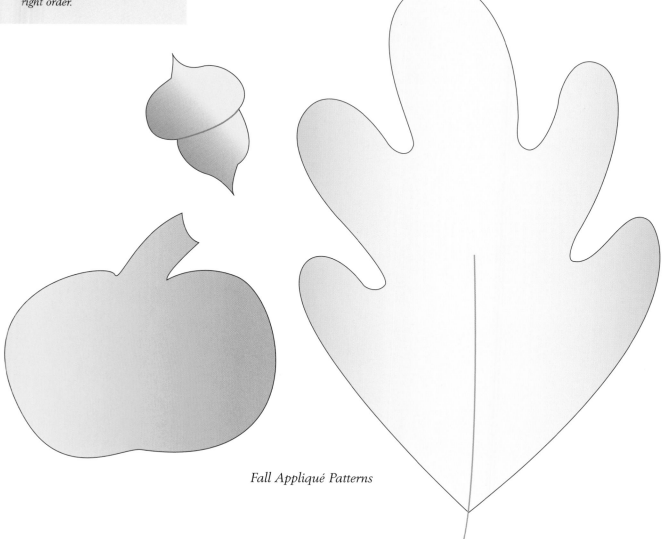

*Fall Appliqué Patterns*

*Summer
Appliqué Patterns*

*Winter
Appliqué Patterns*

*Spring*
*Appliqué Patterns*

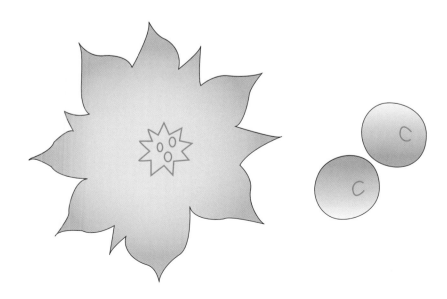

# VIP TRIANGLE
## *Scrap Quilt*

by Debbie Bowles

*Every quilter cringes* at the thought of tossing away scraps. Lots of the leftovers are triangles lopped off in the process of quick-piecing quilt blocks. Debbie has devised a unique, fun method for teaming these very important pieces (VIP) with beautiful threads, fancy stitches, and playful rickrack to make quilts that have movement and interest. The method can be used to create endless designs, playing off the theme and colors of the border and background fabrics you choose.

Wall Hanging
*32" × 26" (81.5 × 66 cm)*
*Machine appliqué, decorative machine stitching,*
*free-motion quilting*

## MATERIALS

¾ yd. (0.7 m) fabric for background

24 to 30 triangles cut from 3¼"
(8.2 cm) squares, in five different
fabrics

Six 1" (2.5 cm) squares of the
triangle fabrics

¼ yd. (0.25 m) fabric for inner
border, in fabric that picks up
the colors of the triangles

½ yd. to ⅝ yd. (0.5 to 0.6 m)
fabric for outer border; more fabric
needed for directional prints

⅜ yd. (0.35 m) fabric for binding

1 yd. (0.92 m) fabric for backing

1 yd. (0.92 m) batting

Narrow masking tape

Lightweight tear-away stabilizer

Decorative threads

Jumbo rickrack, two packages

Monofilament thread and thread
to match rickrack

## DESIGNER'S TIP

*For the triangles to be sharp, choose fabrics with very high contrast. Triangle fabrics with a great deal of background or very busy multicolored prints may be disappointing as they lose their distinct edges. The edging thread will show only if it contrasts with all the fabrics. Blend the thread to the fabrics for a subtle look.*

## Instructions

1   Wash, dry, and press all the fabrics. Shrink the batting according to the manufacturer's directions, if desired.

2   Cut the background panel 26" × 20" (66 × 51 cm). Using narrow masking tape, create a grid on the background to help visualize placement of the design. Place one horizontal strip about 7" (18 cm) from the lower edge; divide the upper section into two equal halves. Secure tear-away stabilizer under the lower section.

3   Arrange 7 to 10 overlapping triangles in the lower section with their bases forming a gradual, moving curve. Overlap the triangles as much as desired to suit your eye and the curve. Allow 3" to 4" (7.5 to 10 cm) at the sides for rickrack to extend.

4   Place the rickrack over the base of the triangles to check that it will lay smoothly over the curve you have created; adjust if necessary. Remove the rickrack, and pin the triangles in place. Trim off any edges that will extend below the base-line curve.

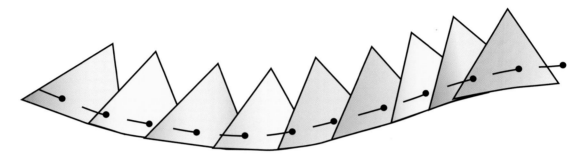

5   Stitch along the two upper sides of the first, undermost triangle, using a zigzag or decorative machine stitch. Begin and end with very short stitches to lock. Lift the edge of the overlapping triangle out of the way as you stitch. Stop stitching just beyond a point that will be covered by the overlapping piece.

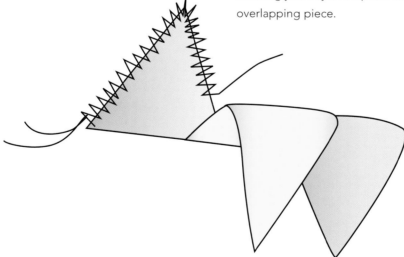

6   Continue stitching the triangles until the row is completed, stitching to the base of the last triangle. Straight stitch along the baseline curve very close to the raw edge.

7   Position the rickrack over the baseline curve, creating loops or swirls at the ends that extend into adjacent areas if desired; pin. Stitch through the center of the rickrack, easing it to lay flat on the surface.

8   Place small fabric squares over the rickrack ends and secure using zigzag or decorative stitches.

9   Create curving designs to fit the remaining two sections, following the same steps. Sharper curves may require more trimming and "fussing" to get them to fit.

10  Carefully remove the stabilizer. Press the quilt top. Trim the quilt top to 24½" × 18½" (62.3 × 47.3 cm).

11  Cut inner border strips 1½" (3.8 cm) wide. Apply two 24½" (62.3 cm) borders to the top and bottom edges; press seam allowances toward the borders. Apply two 20½" (52.3 cm) borders to the side; press seam allowances toward the borders.

12  Cut outer border strips 3½" (9 cm) wide. Apply two 20½" (52.3 cm) outer borders to the sides. Press the seam allowances toward the borders. Apply two 32½" (82.8 cm) borders to the top and bottom; press the seam allowances toward the borders. (Note that the outer borders were cut from a directional print, with top and bottom on the crosswise grain and sides on the lengthwise grain, in order to apply them all facing in the same direction.)

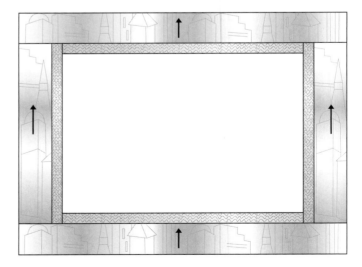

13 Cut backing and batting slightly larger than the quilt top. Layer and baste the backing, batting, and quilt top. Using monofilament thread and a walking foot, stitch in the ditch around the border seams. Then quilt in random, spiky zigzags that echo the angles of the triangles in the spaces around the appliquéd designs. Quilt broad, irregular zigzags in the outer border.

14 Switch to thread the same color as the rickrack. Attach a darning foot, drop or cover the feed dogs, and stitch freehand back and forth on the points of the rickrack.

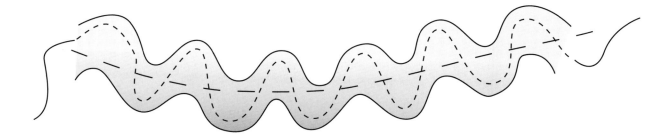

15 Bind the quilt as desired. Attach a sleeve for hanging (page 119).

## DESIGNER'S TIP

*Always measure your quilt top horizontally and vertically through the center and cut border strips to these measurements. The border measurements given in these steps presume a perfectly cut, stitched, and pressed quilt top. Your measurements may be slightly different. Match the center of each border strip to the center of the quilt edge and use pins generously.*

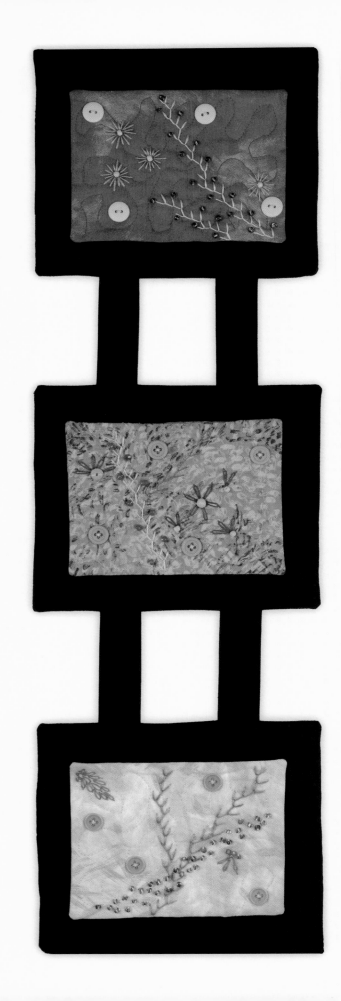

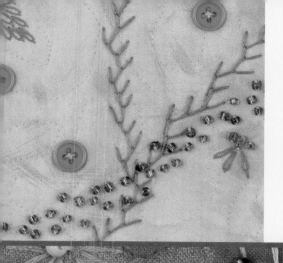

# MINI ART QUILT
## *Wall Hanging*

by Phyllis Dobbs

*The bright colors* of these three mini quilts really pop against their black backgrounds. Phyllis designed and made each separately, then tacked the art quilts onto black fabric frames to form a wall hanging. Hand embroidery, beading, buttons, and free-motion quilting give the quilts dimension and interest. You can follow Phyllis's designs or create mini art quilts that show off your favorite embellishments and handwork.

Wall Hanging
8" × 25½" (20.5 × 64.8 cm)
*Free-motion quilting, embroidery, beadwork*

## DESIGNER'S TIP

*Lay out an assortment of embellishments over the fabrics you select. Note how the colors play off the background fabrics. Pick elements for each section that stand out from their background in vivid contrast while echoing colors from the other backgrounds to unify the set.*

### MATERIALS

½ yd. (0.5 m) black fabric

¼ yd. (0.25 m) bright pink marbled fabric

¼ yd. (0.25 m) bright green marbled fabric

¼ yd. (0.25 m) bright yellow marbled fabric

Four orange buttons

Four turquoise buttons

Four pale green buttons

DMC six-strand cotton embroidery floss, numbers: 3340, 907, 726, and 3804

Turquoise silver-lined rochaille E beads

Green silver-lined rochaille E beads

Orange silver-lined rochaille E beads

Orange opaque E beads

Yellow opaque E beads

Two ¼" (6 mm) yellow opaque beads

½ yd. Warm & Natural® needled cotton batting

Embroidery needle

Sharp scissors

Two small plastic rings

## Instructions

1   Cut six 8½" × 7" (21.8 × 18 cm) rectangles and four 2½" × 3½" (6.5 × 9 cm) rectangles from black fabric. Cut two 6½" × 5" (16.3 × 12.7 cm) rectangles from each of the colored fabrics.

2   Fold a small black rectangle in half lengthwise. Stitch the long edges together, using a ¼" (6 mm) seam allowance. Turn right side out and press so the seam is centered down the back. Repeat for the remaining small black rectangles, making four connecting strips.

3   Pin two large black rectangles, right sides together, over the batting. Repeat for the remaining two black rectangles and the three colored rectangles. Cut out batting to the same size as each set.

4   Unpin the upper edge of one of the black sets. Slip two connecting strips between the fabric layers, seam side up, aligning the raw edges with outer edges 2" (5 cm) from the sides of the large rectangles. Repeat along the lower edge. Stitch the set together, leaving a 3" (7.5 cm) opening along one side. Turn right sides out and press the outer edges. Slipstitch the opening closed. This will be the center frame.

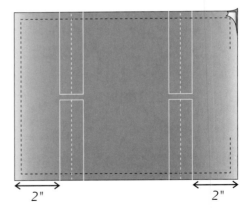

5   Unpin the upper edge of one of the remaining black sets. Fold up the center frame, leaving two connecting strips extending on one side. Slip it between the fabric layers, aligning the raw edges of the strips to the upper edge of the set, seam side up, 2" (5 cm) from the outer edges. Stitch the set together, taking care not to catch the center frame in the stitching; leave a 3" (7.5 cm) opening along one side. Turn right side out and press the outer edges. Slipstitch the opening closed.

6   Unpin the lower edge of the remaining set. Fold up the two completed frames, leaving the two free connecting strips extending. Slip them between the fabric layers and complete the frame, as in step 7.

7   Stitch the pink set together, leaving a 3" (7.5 cm) opening along one side. Turn right side out and press the outer edges. Slipstitch the opening closed. Repeat for the green and yellow sets.

8   Stipple-quilt loosely over each of the colored quilt rectangles, using thread colors to match the backgrounds.

9   Stitch the embroidery stitches on the quilted rectangles, following the key and using three strands of floss. Stitch beads where shown.

10  Pin each mini quilt to its frame. Secure by stitching buttons to the quilts through all layers. Tack invisibly at the corners, if necessary. Stitch plastic rings to the back upper corners for hanging.

**STITCH KEY**

*Feather Stitch*

*Straight Stitch*

*Lazy Daisy*

Instructions for stitches can be found on
pages 54 and 55.

*Mini Quilt Patterns*

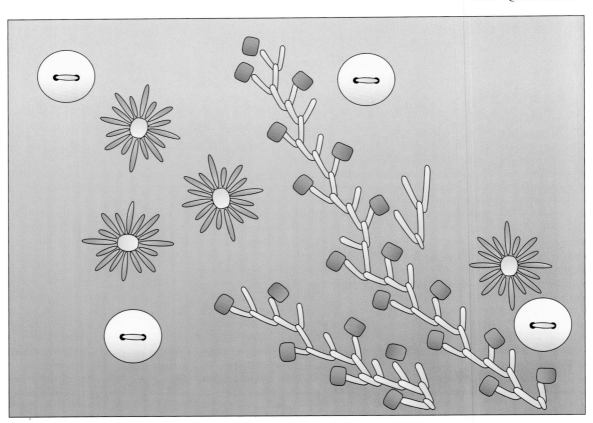

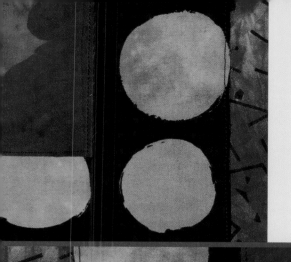

# FAVORITE FABRIC
## *Wall Collage*

by Susan Stein

*Surface design and embellishment* are ways of taking quilting in a more artistic direction. Innovative techniques for coloring, printing, and texturizing fabrics, along with ever-expanding options for decorative threads and trims, provide an infinite variety of materials to use. Susan sells fabulous hand-dyed and hand-printed fabrics in her quilt shop. As wonderful new fabrics are brought in by fabric artists, she collects favorite pieces for her own stash. Making small-scale wall collages gives her an opportunity to showcase a few of these fabrics.

Wall Collage
*27" × 21" (68.5 × 53.5 cm)*
*Fabric collage, raw-edge appliqué*

## MATERIALS

⅔ yd. (0.63 m) fabric
for background

Small pieces of accent fabrics

Sun-printed squares

Screen-printed squares

Rickrack, ribbon, hand-dyed
rayon twill tape, or other trims

Buttons, beads

¼ yd. (0.25 m) binding fabric

⅔ yd. ( 0.63 m) backing fabric

80/20 Hobbs Heirloom® fusible
batting or other lightweight batting

Basting glue or glue stick

Thread

## Instructions

1   Collect the fabrics and trims for the collage. Place all the possible elements on a design wall and view them from a distance to determine whether something is too bold or is the wrong color. Check for contrast between elements, a variety of visual textures, differences in scale if using prints, interesting motifs, and different color values.

2   Cut a rectangle of background fabric. If it is a lightweight or slippery fabric, adhere fusible batting, such as 80/20 Hobbs Heirloom, to the back to stabilize it.

3   Hang the background fabric on the design wall. You may decide at this point to hang the collage vertically or horizontally or you may make that determination later in the design process. The quilt will start to "speak to you" after a while. Take your time in the designing stage.

*Materials Susan used were
hand-dyed by Wendy Richardson,
Diane Swallen, and Diane Bartels.*

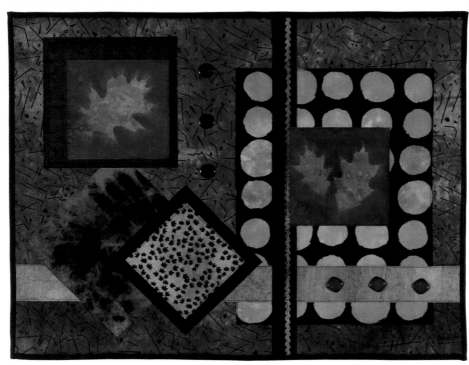

## DESIGNER'S TIP

*Pick a theme or coordinated color scheme to lend unity to the quilt. Leaves, petroglyphs, or a memory might be the starting point for your collection. Pick colors that are next to each other on the color wheel or colors that are opposite each other or different values of the same color. Your quilt will be more pleasing if there is contrast but not too many colors. Black makes a good accent for most colors and can frame an element that blends into the background.*

4  Cut two or three pieces of accent fabric and screen-printed or sun-printed squares to audition on top of the background fabric. Keep the pieces small enough to allow you to use several different ones but avoid cutting pieces that are so small that they don't make a statement. Keep moving the pieces around on the background and stand back from the design wall to evaluate the placement and effectiveness. Eliminate pieces that don't compliment the design and look for pieces that unify the overall effect but don't blend in too much. Overlap pieces and orient some of them vertically, some horizontally, some on point. Repetition of some elements adds unity to a design and carries the eye around the quilt. If you like lots of texture, choose pieces that ravel readily, like loosely woven cotton or silk dupioni. If you don't like raveled edges, choose tightly woven pima cotton, silk noile, or try silk habotai with the edges singed in a candle flame.

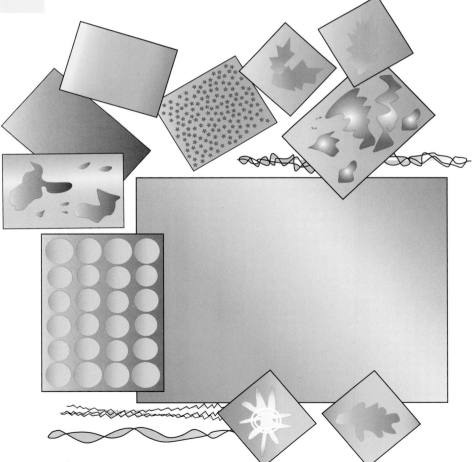

5   Cut two or three long strips of various widths and fabrics and add them horizontally and vertically, sometimes going over the other pieces and sometimes slipping under them. They can extend from edge to edge or stop in the middle of the quilt. Try cutting a strip into sections and leaving spaces between them or end a strip and then add three squares to the space beyond the end.

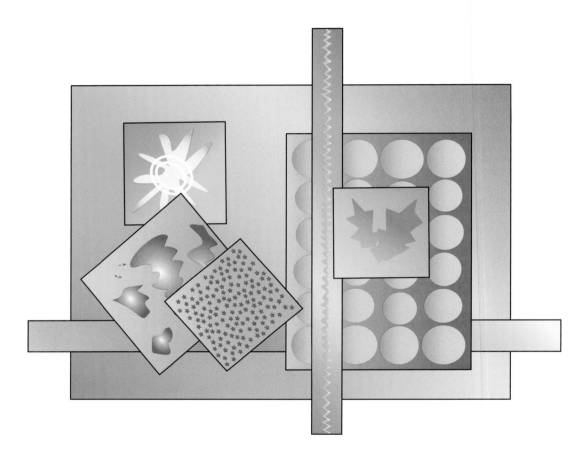

6   Straighten and trim the edges of all the pieces, if you haven't already done so, and then pin in place. Remove the quilt from the wall.

7   Use basting glue or glue stick to lightly adhere the pieces to the background.

8   If you haven't used fusible batting for stabilizer, add the batting and backing to the quilt top. If the quilt has been stabilized, just add backing. Pin-baste the layers together.

9   Quilt around the edges of all the pieces about ⅛" (3 mm) from the raw edges. Use contrasting or variegated thread to add interest. Stitch "casual straight lines" to quilt large open areas on the accent pieces. Quilt around printed motifs if you wish. Keep the quilting consistent on all areas of the quilt so it doesn't pucker up in one spot and appear too puffy in others. Double-stitch accent pieces that tend to ravel a lot to protect the edges. When starting and ending a line of stitching, use very tiny stitches to secure the thread.

10   If you are using twill tape, ribbon, or rickrack, lay that on the quilt and stitch over it. To add dimension and texture, quilt down the middle. If you prefer a neater appearance, quilt down both sides of the ribbon or tape.

11   Bind the quilt with 2" (5 cm) wide strips. Make a sleeve for hanging. Pin it to the back upper edge; hand-stitch in place.

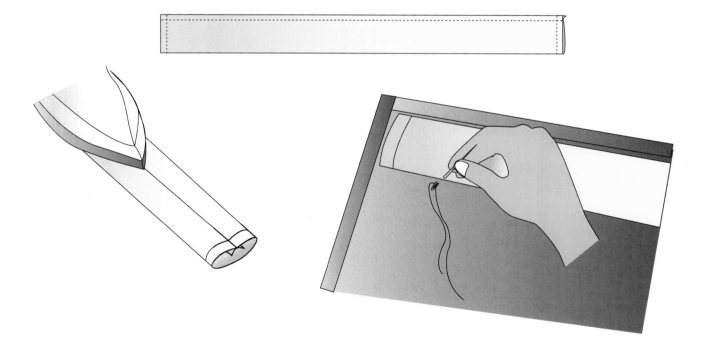

12   Steam the quilt to block it.

13   Add the buttons and beads. Sign your name on the quilt. Proudly display it as your one-of-a-kind creation.

# QUILT DESIGNERS
## *Who Sometimes Think Small*

*Denise Bielick* designs patterns for quilting, needlework, and other textile related areas under the company name Oak Hill Designs. She enjoys all types of quilting, sewing, and embroidery. The natural scenery and wildlife on her wooded acreage in southeastern Minnesota are daily inspirations for her designs. As a member of the Society of Craft Designers (SCD), Denise has taught and demonstrated in the areas of quilting and needlework for eight years. From her web site www.oakhilldesigns.com, Denise sells fine needlework and quilting supplies and patterns, specializing in embellishments and hand-painted or dyed, often one-of-a-kind fabrics. In her free time, Denise loves to garden, and she hopes that one day she will actually have flower beds and vegetable gardens that resemble the ones in the gardening magazines, rather than glorified weed patches. Perhaps her time will come when her teenage children have graduated from high school and gone off to college.

*Debbie Bowles* is the owner of Maple Island Quilts, a pattern line of high impact, slightly nontraditional patterns for quilters of all skill levels. Once an elementary school teacher, she now teaches and lectures about quilting throughout the country at shops, guild meetings and quilting events, having fun helping her students create achievable projects that are uniquely their own. Debbie will be a frequent guest on the new PBS quilting show, "M'Liss's World of Quilts." In addition to her pattern line, Debbie has written two books, *Cutting Curves from Straight Pieces* and *Dancing Quilts from Straight Pieces*. Her patterns and workshop schedule can be viewed on her web site: www.mapleislandquilts.com.

*Barbara Boyd* has always loved fabric and sewing. Her grandmother was her mentor and taught her to sew when she was a little girl. By the age of twelve she was sewing her own clothes. Quilting caught her fancy in 1978, when Barbara soon learned that hand quilting, hand appliqué, and embellishments were her passion. For fifteen years, she has taught quilting in shops, shows, and quilt guild meetings while continuing to take advanced classes herself. "There is always something new to learn," she reminds us.

*Janis Bullis* has been serving the home decorating and craft industries for more than twenty years as a consultant and designer. Her clients include book, magazine, and pattern publishers, as well as craft and textile manufacturers. Janis is often asked to design prototypes, or very first patterns, for bed linen, gift, and other manufacturers who need to know how size, shape, color, and texture will impact the final look and production of an item before millions are produced. Alone and with others, Janis has contributed as author, editor, and designer to more than 100 how-to publications whose topics range from bridal accouterments and baby accessories to holiday decorating. Her favorite media are fabric and trims. She is also a frequent contributor to well-known women's magazines. Her overall goal is to help consumers enjoy the benefits and rewards of creative sewing and crafts.

*Patricia Converse* is a long-time artist, crafter, and avid quilter. Sewing, textiles, fiber arts, and fine crafts have always been her loves. Her designs are inspired by the natural setting of her rural Pennsylvania home, where she works and lives with her husband and four children. As an SCD member, she is also an author and teacher, with a degree in home economics. Because quilting is such a varied handcraft, Patricia enjoys designing projects that leave themselves open to individualization.

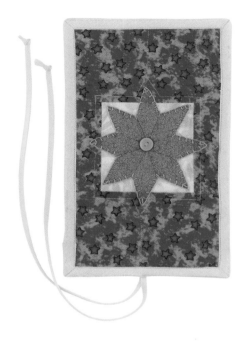

*Phyllis Dobbs* began stitching at a very early age and was taught needlework, sewing, quilting, and crochet by her mother and aunt. She gained a great love and appreciation for quilting from her grandmother's and great-grandmother's quilts, which she safeguards in her home. She earned a BS degree in Interior Design from the University of Alabama, her home state, and is also an SCD member. Inspired by her love of needlework, Phyllis began designing professionally in 1984 and formed her own company, Lucky Duck Designs. In the next six years, she self-published 49 counted cross stitch leaflets and books. Then, in 1990, Phyllis began designing quilts and now has over 1000 published needlework and quilt designs. Her design studio, which occupies the second floor of her home, is a collage of fabrics, fibers, beads, buttons, and wonderful assortments of inspirational materials. Her web site is: www.phyllisdobbs.com.

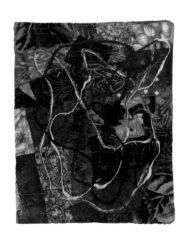

*Karen Bailey Earith*, a fiber artist living in Knoxville, Tennessee, writes for several publications and teaches extensively. Since becoming an occupational therapist in 1983, she has been teaching people with disabilities how to create art. She believes in helping everyone reach his or her creative potential, regardless of age or skill level. Karen enjoys creating art quilts and wearables that have visual and/or actual textural elements. These elements often include beads, buttons, hand-painted fabric, manipulated fabric, cords, yarns, and found objects. Karen hopes her work, which has been seen nationally, will give viewers a sense of joy and well-being.

*Laura Murray* discovered the enduring passion of her life—the art quilt—in 1989, after spending the previous 20 years doing various forms of needlework. This passion began a journey through experimentation with color and texture that continues unabated to this day. Her quilts have been exhibited internationally in major quilt shows and galleries and have

won numerous awards, including Best Wall Quilt from the American Society of Quilters in Paducah, Kentucky; Best of Show in the Mid-Atlantic Quilt Festival; and first place in the Houston International Quilt Festival. Laura is the owner of Laura Murray Designs, which offers an elegant and whimsical collection of fabrics, stencils, patterns, stamps, buttons, foils, and textile art supplies at quilt and sewing shows across the U.S. She is an author, teacher, and designer of a new line of stencils for fabric. Laura's art quilts and wearables can be viewed on her web site: www.lauramurraydesigns.com.

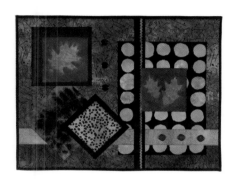

*Susan Stein* has been quilting since 1977, when she threw out all the other needle arts and dove into piles of fabric and stacks of quilt books. Since then, several hundred projects have been completed, to be used for publications, store samples, walls, beds, gifts, commissions, teaching, and lecturing. She currently owns a quilt shop in St. Paul, Minnesota, called Colorful Quilts and Textiles. As an author of two books, Susan frequently focuses on contemporary quilts in collage style, Double Wedding Ring patterns, and sampler-style quilts. In 2003, Susan was voted the Minnesota Quilter of the Year.

*Julann Windsperger* is a nurse by profession, but her real loves are fiber arts and quilting. She creates hand-dyed and painted fabrics, which she turns into one-of-a-kind quilted garments and home décor items. Her unique, complex cloths have been purchased by a German artist. Especially talented at hand-guided machine quilting, Julann was commissioned to work her magic on a quilt that Oprah Winfrey gave to her dear friend Maya Angelou for her 75th birthday. Twice her original quilted garments have won first place ribbons at the Minnesota State Fair. Julann has created designs and written instructions for several publications and teaches wearable art classes at her local quilt shops.

# Sources

Stitchitize Embroidery Design Service
1-800-667-2587
www.stitchitize.com
*Supplier of stock designs and digitizing for computerized embroidery sewing machines.*

June Tailor
www.junetailor.com
*Manufacturer of computer-printable fabric; check for information and dealer locations.*

Fire Mountain Gems and Beads
One Fire Mountain Way
Grants Pass, Oregon 97526-2373
1-800-423-2319
www.firemountaingems.com
*Supplier of beads.*

The Warm™ Company
www.warmcompany.com
*Manufacturer of Warm and Natural® needled cotton batting and Steam-A-Seam® 2 fusible web; check for information and dealer locations.*

Paper Creations
1500 West Rogers Avenue
Appleton, WI 54914
www.papercreations.com
*Supplier of tri-fold window cards.*

Rubber Nature Stamps
7500 125th Avenue
Kenosha, WI 53142
www.rubbernature.com
*Rubber stamps by Sandi Obertin.*

D'UVA Fine Artists Materials
www.duva.com
*Manufacturer of Chroma Coal™ Powder Pigments; check for information and dealer locations.*

Colorful Quilts and Textiles
www.colorfulquilts.com
*Supplier of hand-dyed fabrics by Diane Bartels, Diane Swallen, and Wendy Richardson.*

# Index

# BOOKS FOR QUILTERS
## *from Creative Publishing international*

**Look for these inspiring and informative books at your local quilt shops, fabric and craft stores, and bookstores.**

### *The Quilter's Companion*
The Complete Guide to Machine and Hand Quilting

### *The Quilting Bible*
from the Singer Sewing Reference Library

### *The New Quilting by Machine*
from the Singer Sewing Reference Library

### *Quilts in Bloom*
A Garden of Inspiring Quilts and Techniques with Floral Designs

### *Quilting 101*
A Beginner's Guide to Quilting

### *Ribbon Artistry*
20 Original Projects by Noted Designers

### *Exploring Textile Arts*
The Ultimate Guide to Manipulating, Coloring, and Embellishing Fabrics